**AUTHENTIC TRANSCRIPTIONS
WITH NOTES AND TABLATURE**

relient K

two lefts don't make a right ...but three do

Music transcriptions by Pete Billmann and David Stocker

ISBN 0-634-06641-2

7777 W. BLUEMOUND RD. P.O. BOX 13819 MILWAUKEE, WI 53213

Visit Hal Leonard Online at
www.halleonard.com

Chapstick, Chapped Lips and Things Like Chemistry

Words and Music by Matt Thiessen

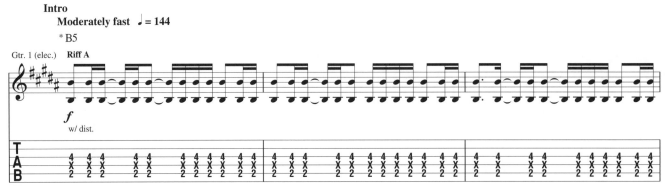

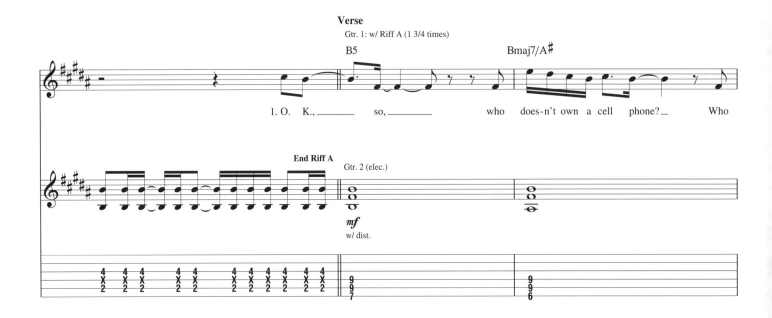

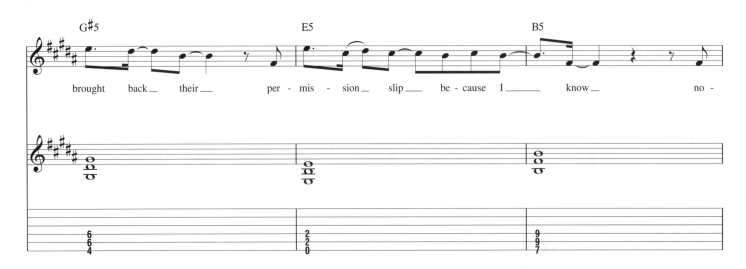

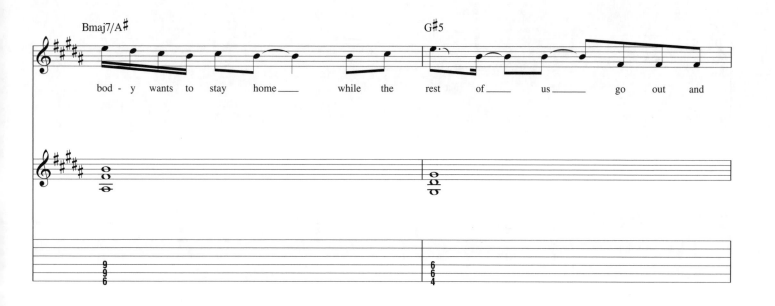

fun when the sun's out - side. _____

sun's out - side.

And I lost _____ my phone to the

Na, na, _____ na, na, na. 'Neath the

lake un-der-neath the Bat-man__ ride.__

Bat - man ride. Na, na,__ na, na.)

End Voc. Fig. 1

End Rhy. Fig. 1

End Rhy. Fig. 1A

Chorus

Gtr. 1: w/ Riff A (3 times)

They're start-ing some-thing and I don't want__ to be-gin____ it.____
(I don't__ wan -

Gtr. 2 Rhy. Fig. 2

*Voc. Fig. 2

*Bkgd. vocs. only

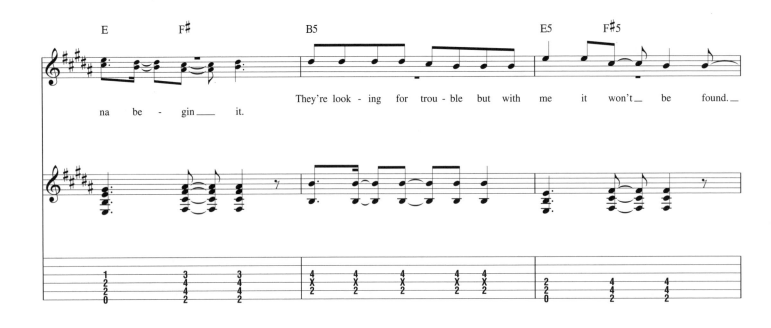

They're look-ing for trou-ble but with me it won't be found.
na be - gin it.

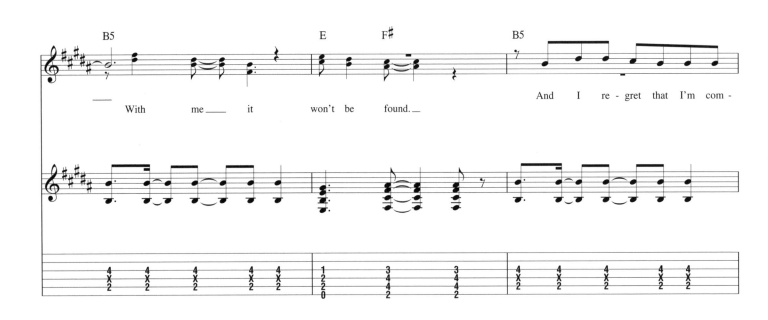

With me it won't be found.
And I re-gret that I'm com-

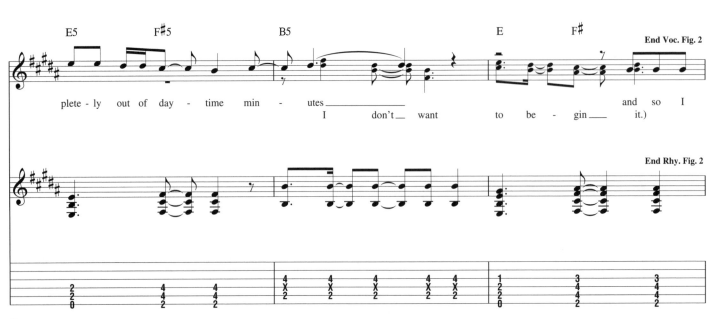

plete-ly out of day-time min-utes
I don't want to be-gin it.)

and so I

End Voc. Fig. 2

End Rhy. Fig. 2

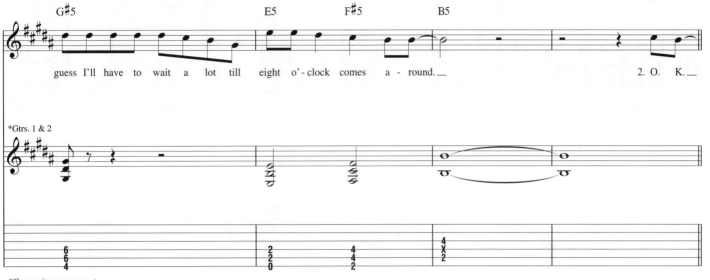

*Composite arrangement

Verse

Gtr. 1: w/ Rhy. Fill 1

Bkgd. Voc.: w/ Voc. Fig. 1
Gtrs. 1 & 2: w/ Rhy. Figs. 1 & 1A

thanks to ___ all ___ those nights and week - ends. 'Cause theme parks are so much ___ more

fun when the sun's out - side. ___ And I lost ___ my phone to the

Chorus

Bkgd. Voc.: w/ Voc. Fig. 2
Gtr. 1: w/ Riff A (3 times)
Gtr. 2: w/ Rhy. Fig. 2

lake be - neath the Bat - man ___ ride. ___ *Spoken:* (Yeah.) They're start - ing some - thing and

I don't want ___ to be - gin ___ it. ___ They're look - ing for trou - ble but with

me it won't ___ be found. ___ And I re - gret that I'm com -

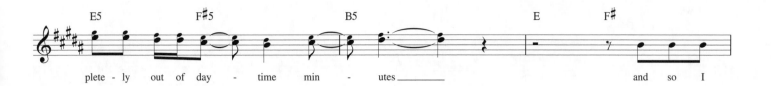

plete - ly out of day - time min - utes _____ and so I

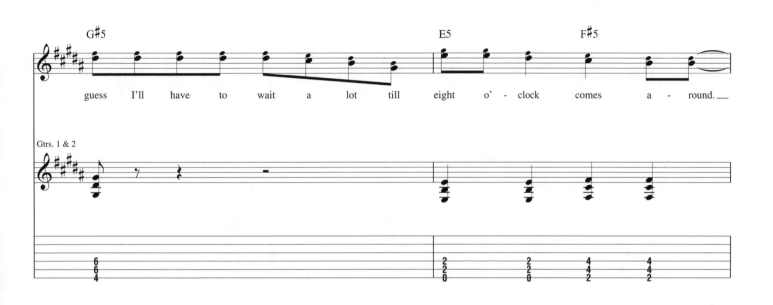

guess I'll have to wait a lot till eight o' - clock comes a - round. ___

Gtrs. 1 & 2

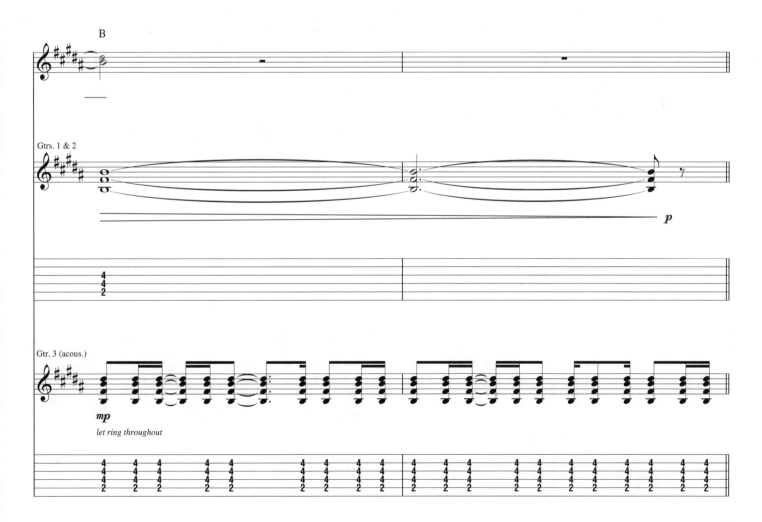

Gtrs. 1 & 2

Gtr. 3 (acous.)

mp

let ring throughout

Bridge

When it comes to re-la-tion-ships (I'm the dumb-est

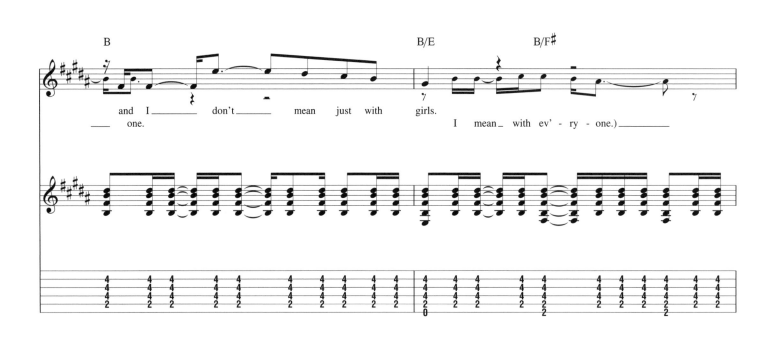

and I don't mean just with girls. one. I mean with ev'-ry-one.)

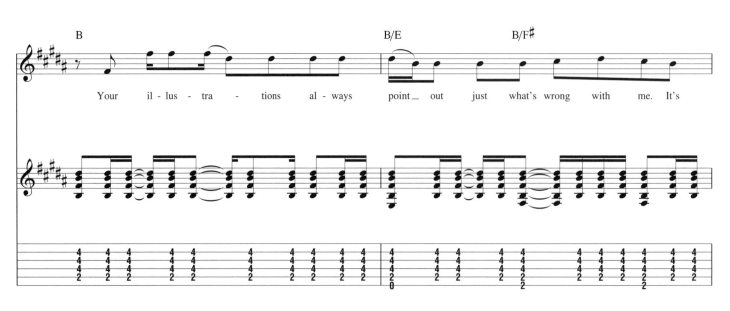

Your il-lus-tra-tions al-ways point out just what's wrong with me. It's

chap - stick___ and chapped lips,___ and things like chem - is - try.

It's chap - stick___ and chapped lips ____ and

things like, ___ it's things like ____ chem - is - try. _____

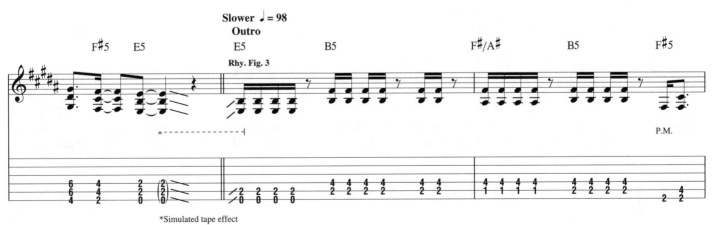

*Simulated tape effect

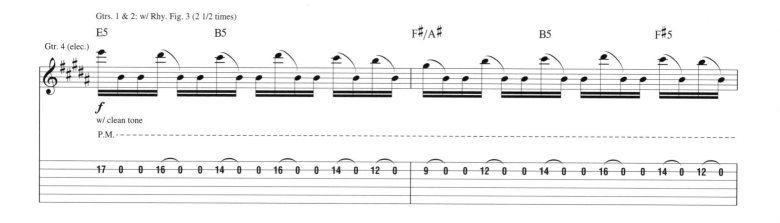

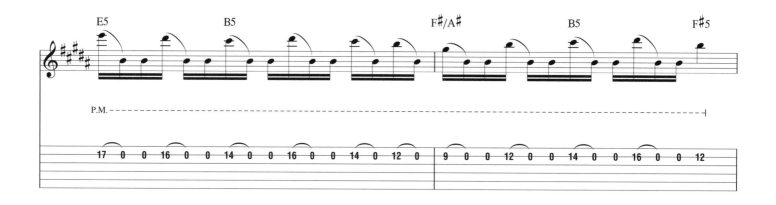

Can I ___ re - late to you the way ___ you ___ re - late to

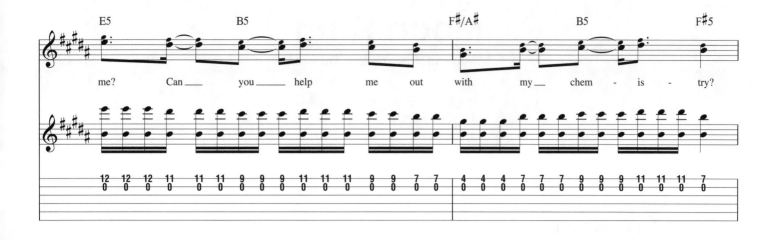

me? Can ___ you ___ help me out with my ___ chem - is - try?

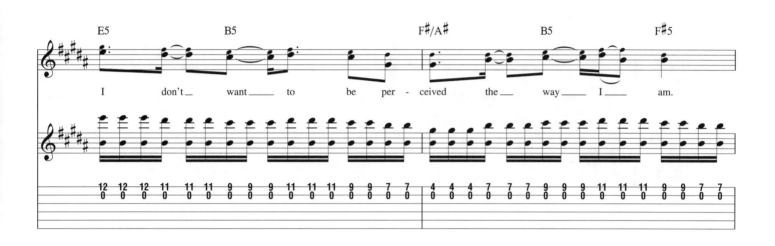

I don't ___ want ___ to be per - ceived the ___ way ___ I ___ am.

I just ___ want ___ to be per - ceived the ___ way ___ I ___ am. ___

Mood Ring

Words and Music by Matt Thiessen

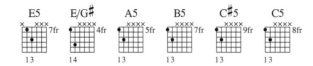

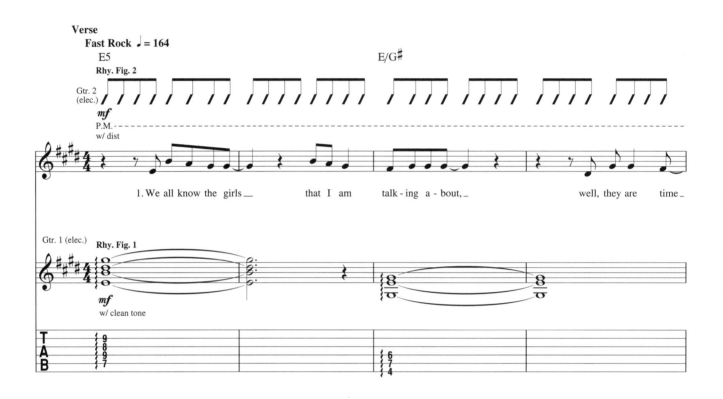

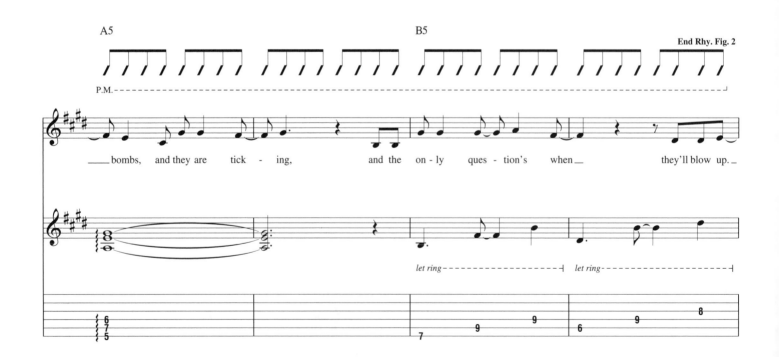

Gtr. 2: w/ Rhy. Fig. 2 (1st 7 meas.)

* Emaj7   E/G#

And they'll blow up, we know_ that with - out a doubt,_   'cause they're those girls_

*Chord symbols reflect overall harmony.

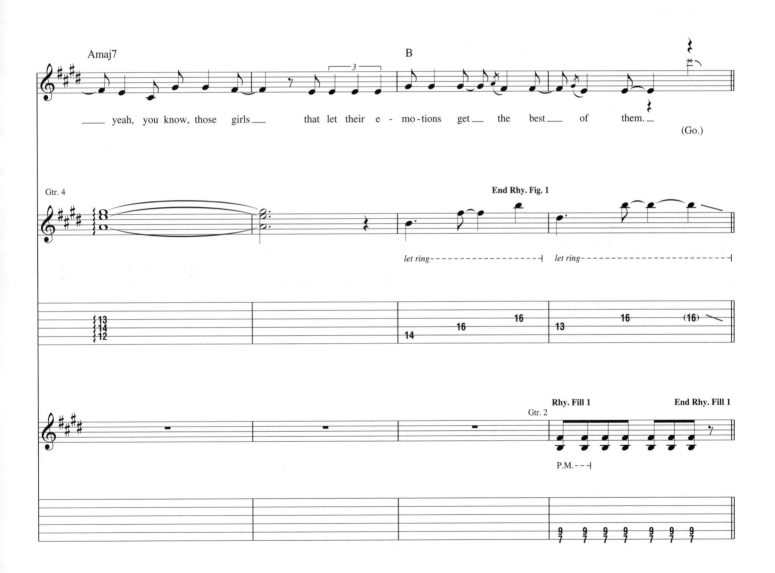

Amaj7   B

_ yeah, you know, those girls_   that let their e - mo-tions get_ the best_ of them._

(Go.)

Gtr. 4

End Rhy. Fig. 1

let ring-----------------   let ring-----------------------

Rhy. Fill 1   End Rhy. Fill 1

Gtr. 2

P.M.- - -

⅜ Pre-Chorus

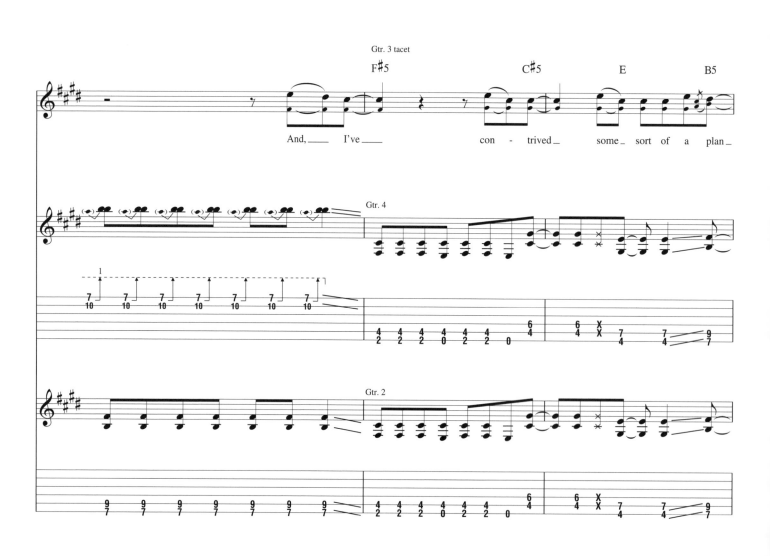

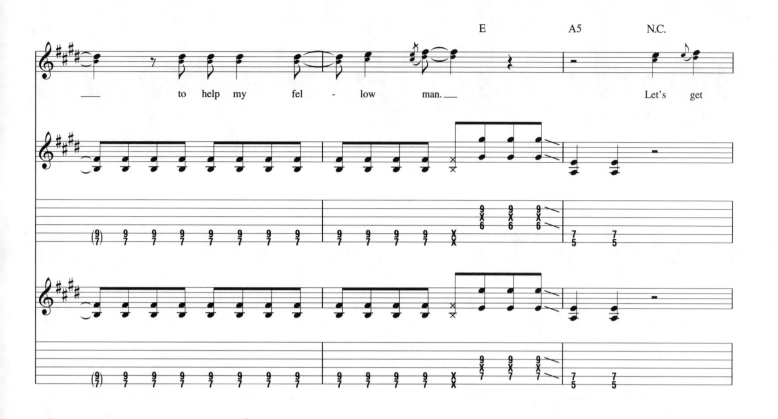

to help my fel - low man.___ Let's get

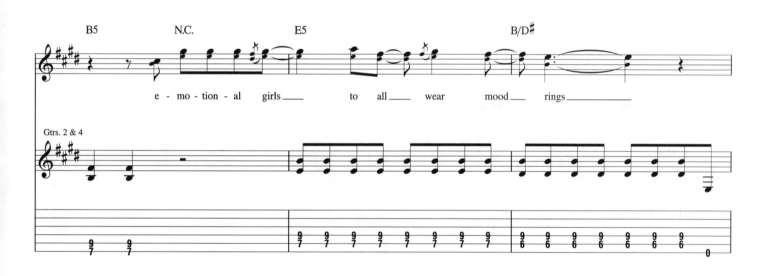

e - mo - tion - al girls___ to all___ wear mood___ rings_____

Gtrs. 2 & 4

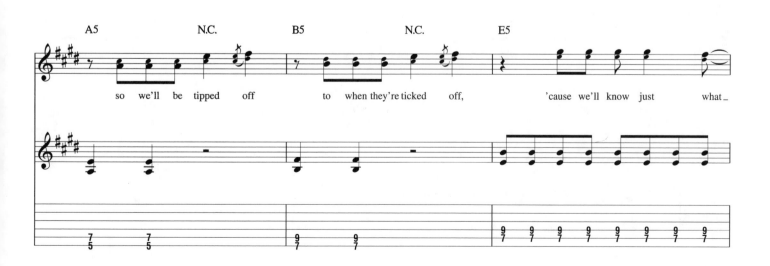

so we'll be tipped off to when they're ticked off, 'cause we'll know just what___

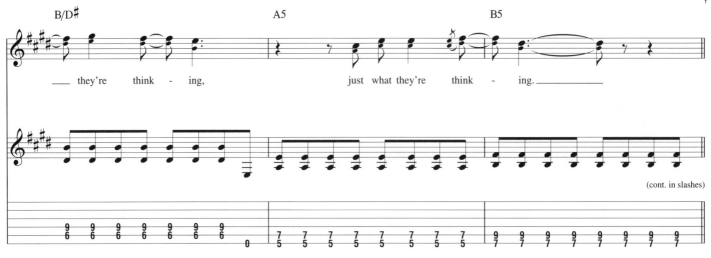

they're think - ing, just what they're think - ing.

(cont. in slashes)

Chorus

She's so pret-ty but she does-n't al-ways act that way. Her moods are swing-in' on the swing set al-most ev-'ry day.

Gtr. 5 (elec.)

mf
w/ dist.

Gtrs. 2 & 4: w/ Rhy. Fig. 3
Gtr 5: w/ Riff A

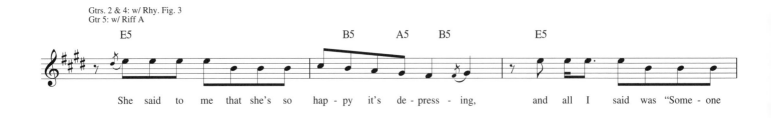

She said to me that she's so hap - py it's de - press - ing, and all I said was "Some - one

Verse

get that girl a mood ring." 2. If it's dra - ma you want, then look no far - ther.

*Chord symbols implied by bass, next 8 meas.

A5

They're like "The Real World" meets "Boy Meets World"

Gtr. 2: w/ Rhy. Fig. 2 (1st 7 meas.)

B5   E5

meets "Days of Our Lives." And it just kills

E/G#

me how they get a - way with mur - der, they'll an - ger you,

A5   B5

then bat their eyes, those pret - ty eyes that watch you sym -

⊕ Coda

D.S. al Coda   **Chorus**

Gtr. 2: w/ Rhy. Fill 1   Gtrs. 2 & 4: w/ Rhy. Fig. 3 (2 times)
                              Gtr. 5: w/ Riff A (2 times)

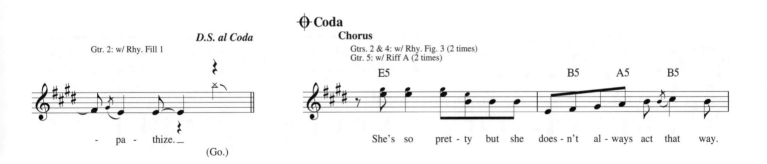

                              E5   B5   A5   B5

- pa - thize.   She's so pret - ty but she does - n't al - ways act that way.

(Go.)

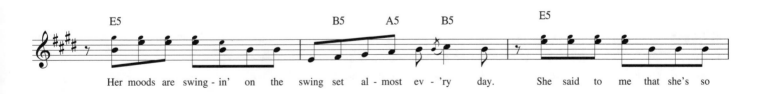

E5   B5   A5   B5   E5

Her moods are swing - in' on the swing set al - most ev - 'ry day. She said to me that she's so

B5   A5   B5   E5   B5   A5   B5

stressed out that it's sooth - ing, and all I said was "Some - one get that girl a mood ring."

Bridge

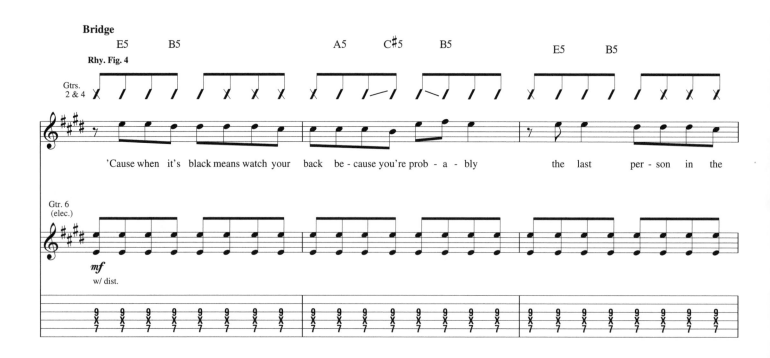

'Cause when it's black means watch your back be-cause you're prob-a-bly the last per-son in the

Gtrs. 2 & 4: w/ Rhy. Fig. 4

world right now she wants to see. And when it's blue it means that you should call her up im-me-di-ate-

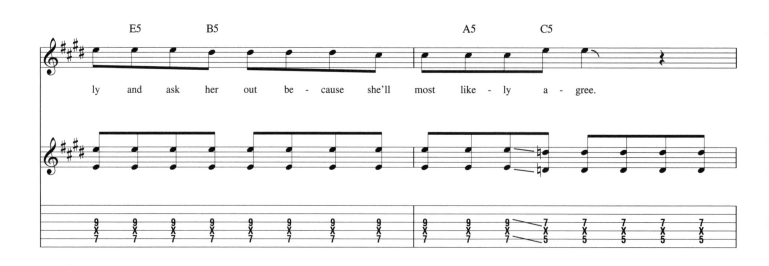

ly and ask her out be-cause she'll most like-ly a-gree.

And when it's green it sim - ply means that she is real - ly stressed. And when it's clear it means she's

com - plete - ly e - mo - tion - less and that's al - right, I must con - fess.

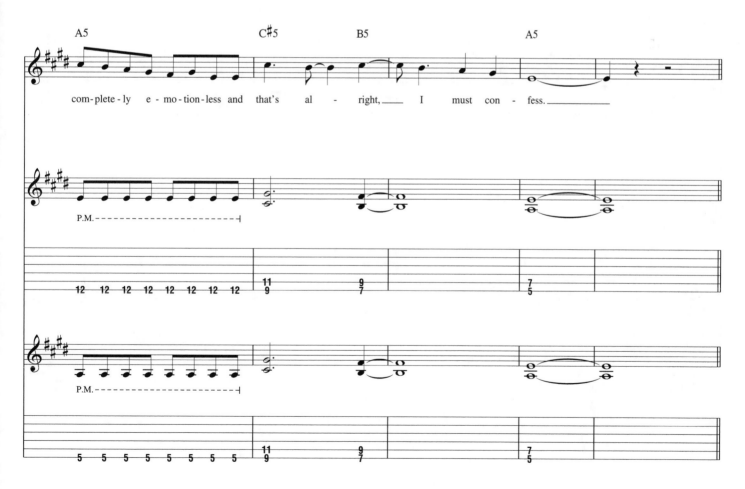

Verse

Gtr. 2: w/ Rhy. Fig. 2 (2 times)
Gtr. 4: w/ Rhy. Fig. 1

We all know the girls___ that I am talk-ing a-bout, she liked you Wednes-

-day, but now it's Fri - day, and she has to wash___ her hair.___

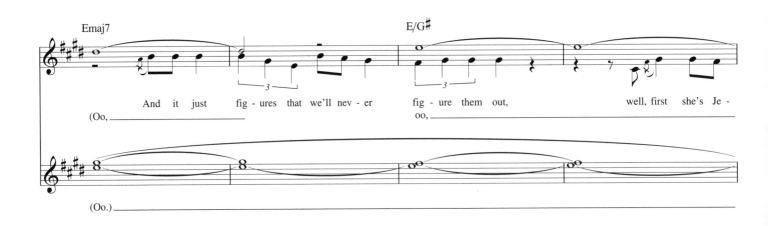

And it just fig - ures that we'll nev - er fig - ure them out, well, first she's Je -
(Oo,___ oo,___

(Oo.)___

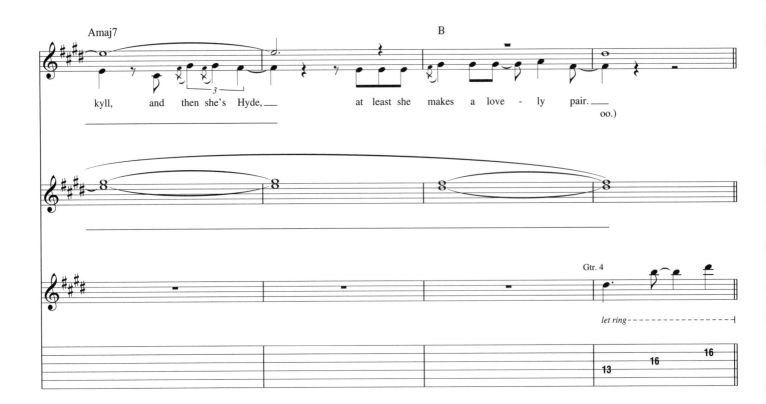

kyll, and then she's Hyde,___ at least she makes a love - ly pair.___
oo.)

Gtr. 4

let ring - - - - - - - - - - - - - - - -

22

Outro
Slower ♩ = 87

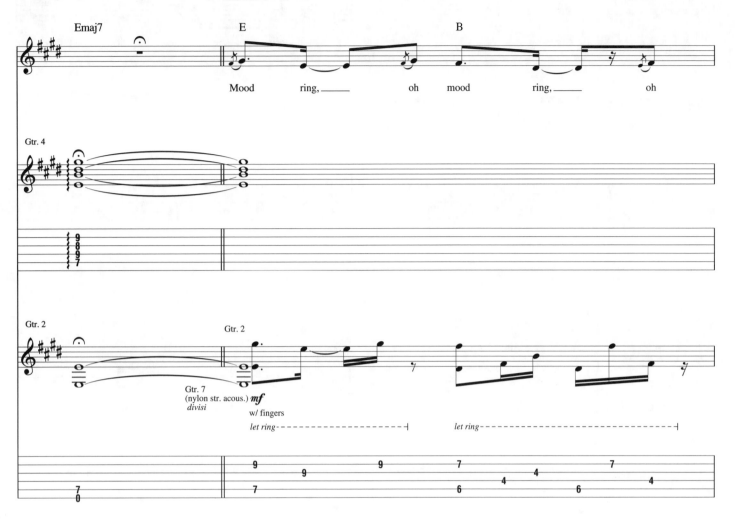

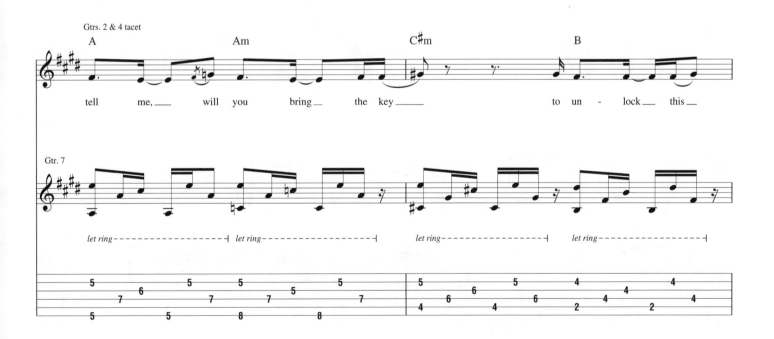

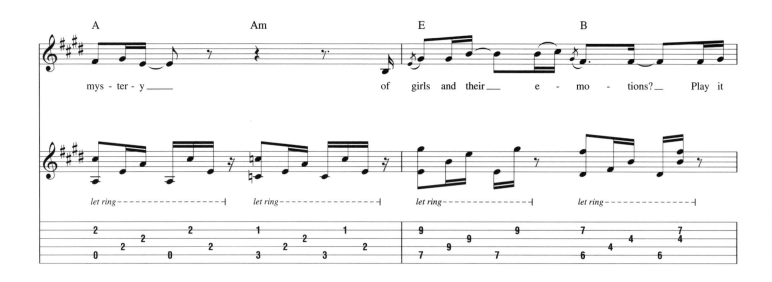

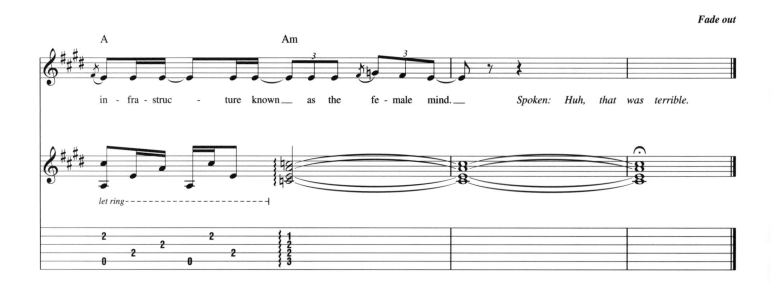

Falling Out

Words and Music by Matt Thiessen

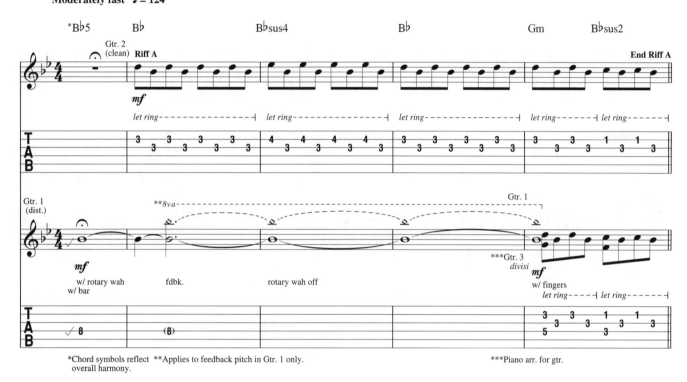

*Chord symbols reflect **Applies to feedback pitch in Gtr. 1 only.
overall harmony.   ***Piano arr. for gtr.

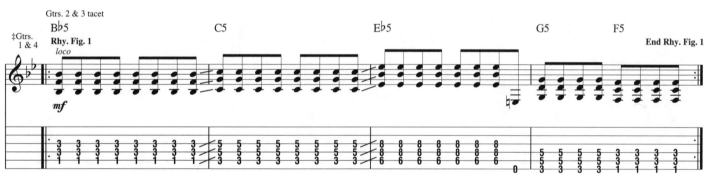

‡Composite arrangement; Gtr. 4 w/ dist.

Verse

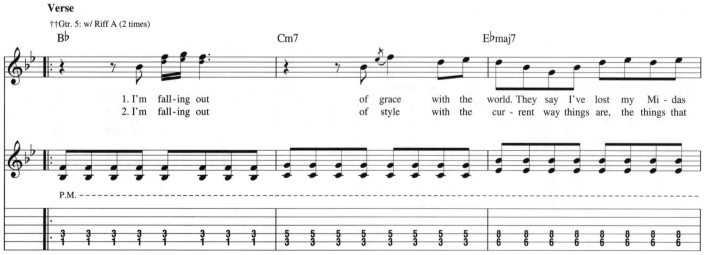

1. I'm fall-ing out   of grace   with the   world. They say I've lost my Mi-das
2. I'm fall-ing out   of style   with the   cur-rent way things are,   the things that

††Gtr. 5 *mf* w/ dist.

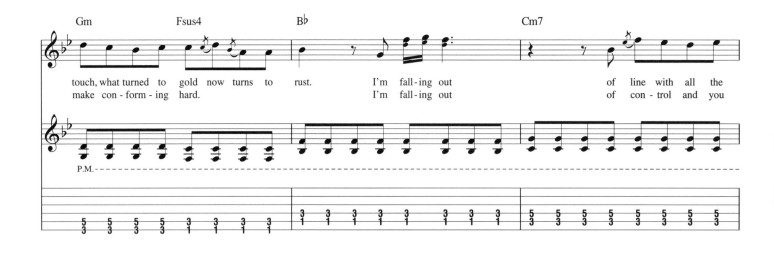

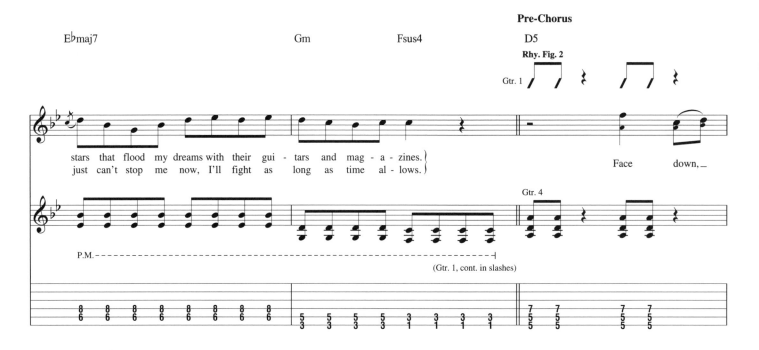

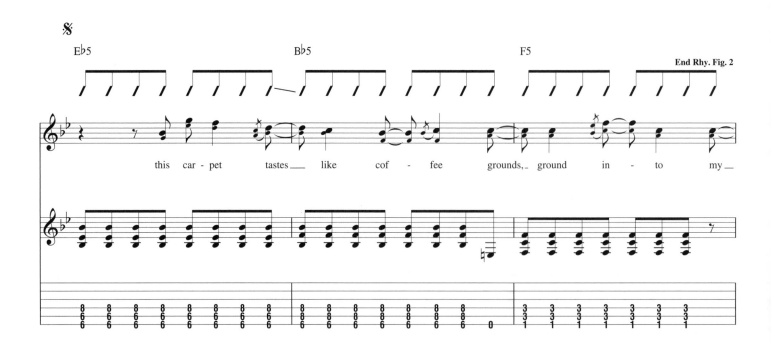

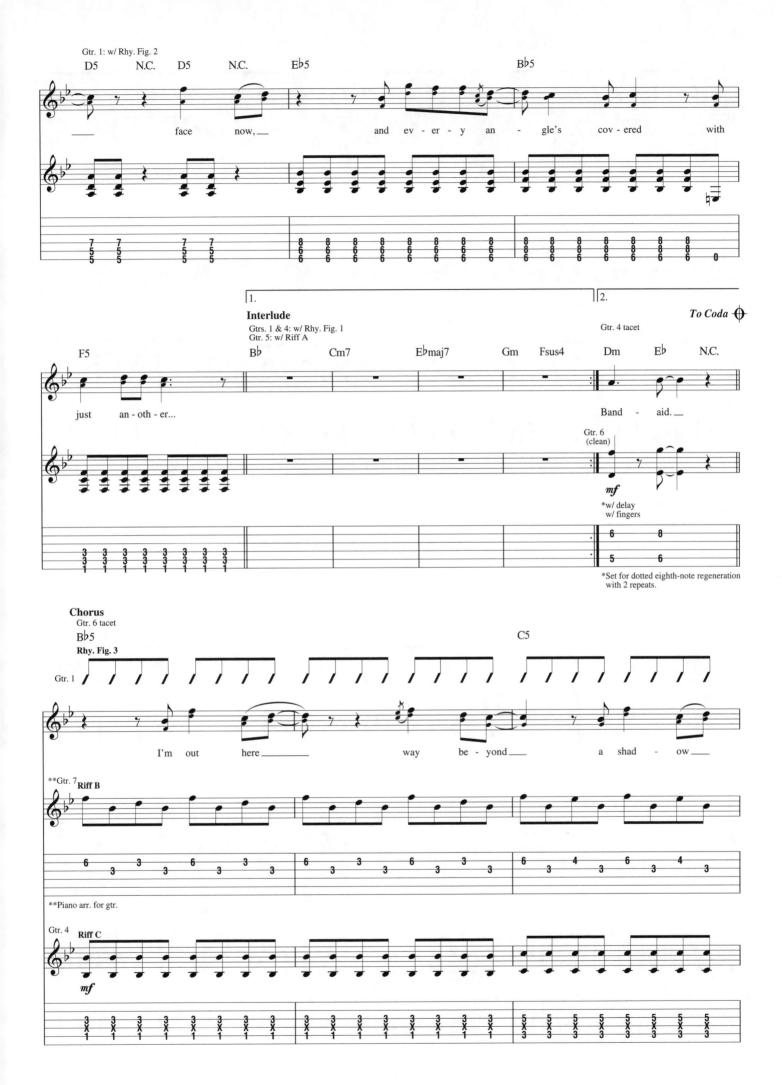

28

Interlude

*Piano arr. for gtr.

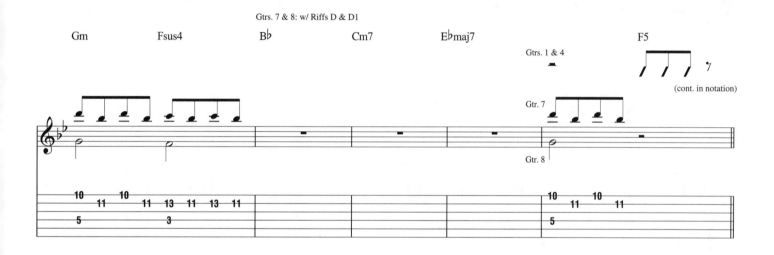

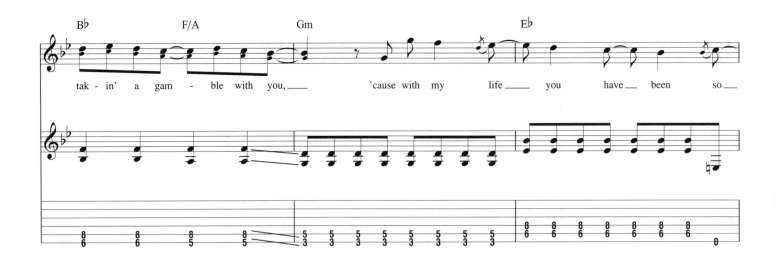

tak - in' a gam - ble with you, _____ 'cause with my life _____ you have _____ been so

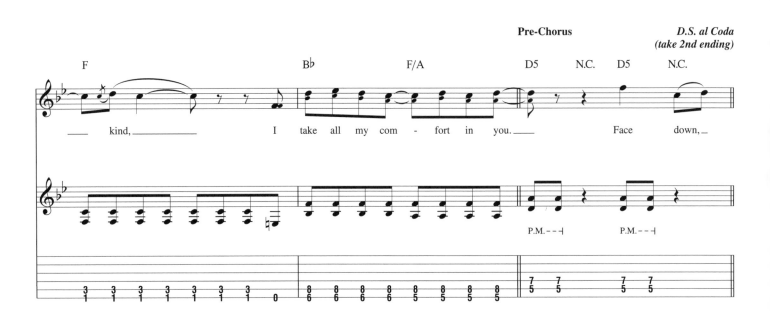

_____ kind, _____ I take all my com - fort in you. _____ Face down, _____

Coda

Chorus
Gtr. 1: w/ Rhy. Fig. 3 (1 3/4 times)
Gtr. 4: w/ Riff C

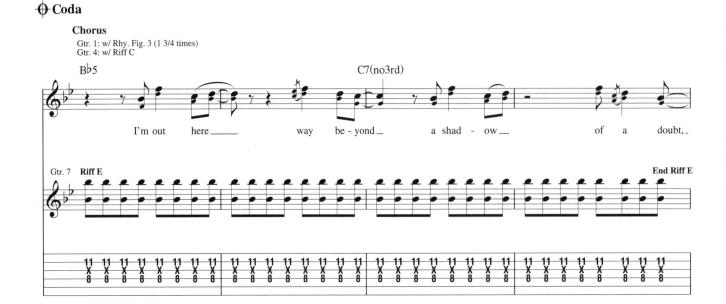

I'm out here _____ way be - yond _____ a shad - ow _____ of a doubt, _____

Gtr. 7 **Riff E**

End Riff E

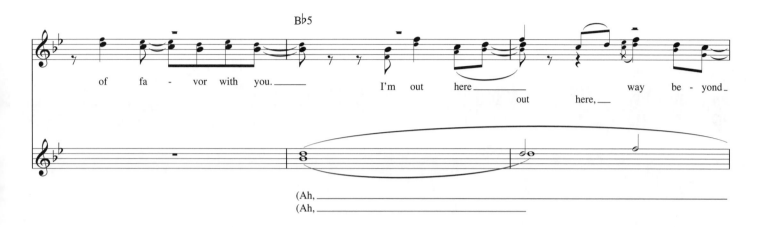

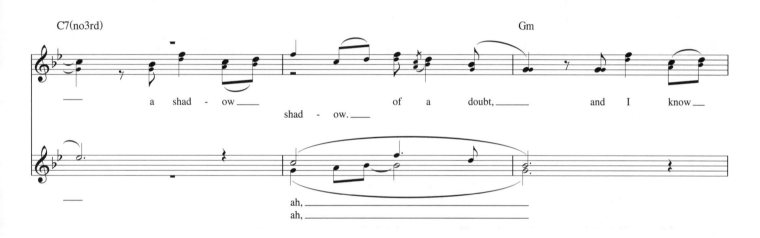

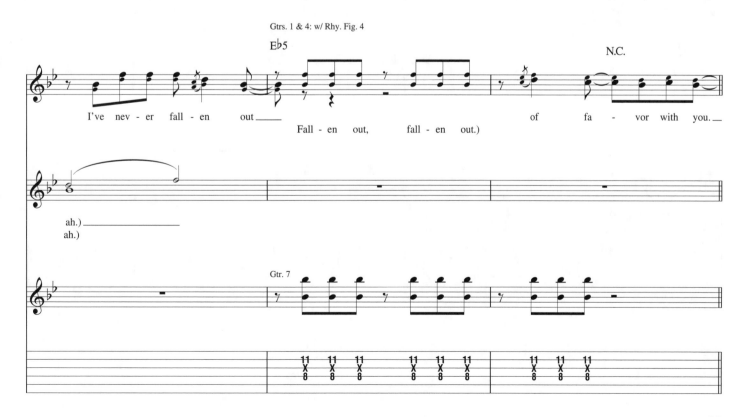

Outro

Gtrs. 1 & 4: w/ Rhy. Fig. 1 (1 1/2 times)
Gtr. 2: w/ Riff A (1 1/2 times)
Gtr. 7: w/ Riff E (2 times)

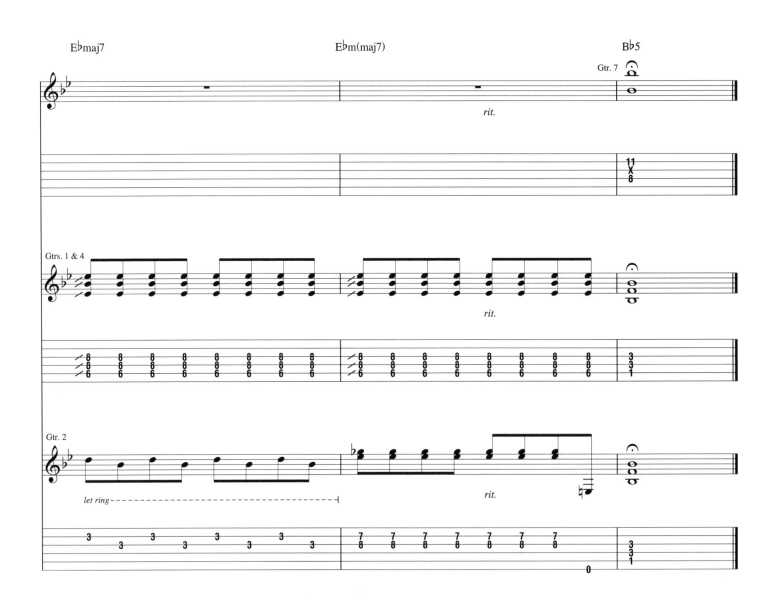

Forward Motion

Words and Music by Matt Thiessen

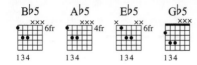

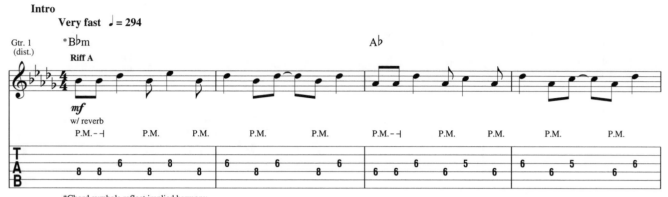

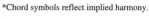

Intro

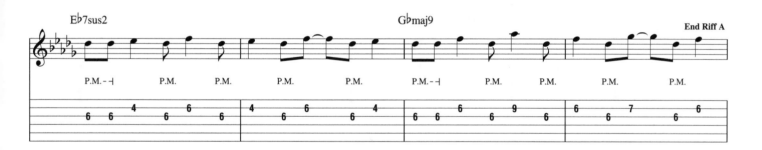

*Chord symbols reflect implied harmony.

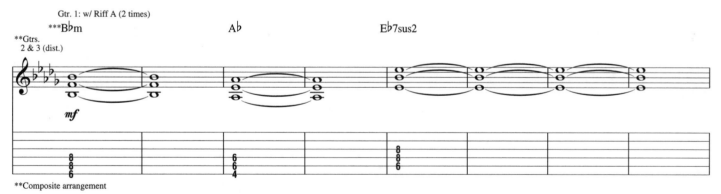

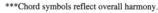

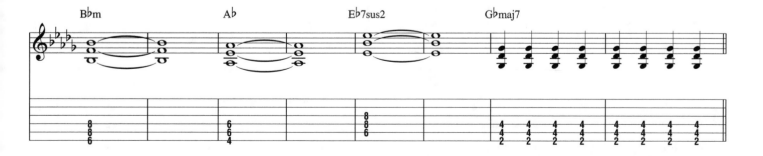

**Composite arrangement

***Chord symbols reflect overall harmony.

Pre-Chorus

Coda 1

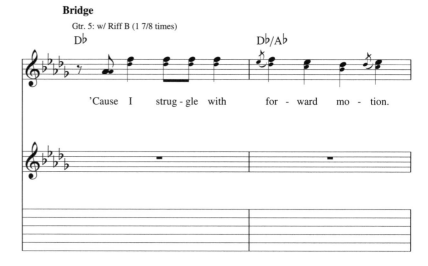

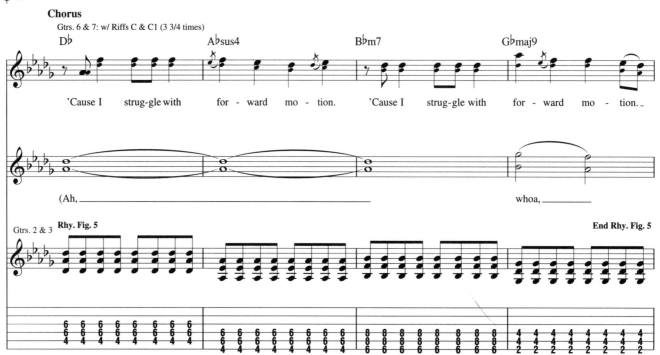

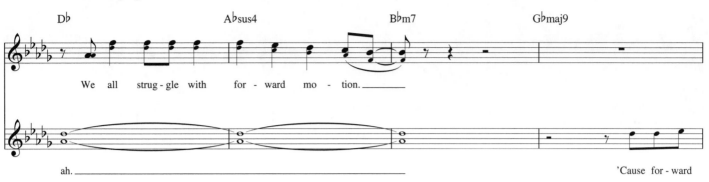

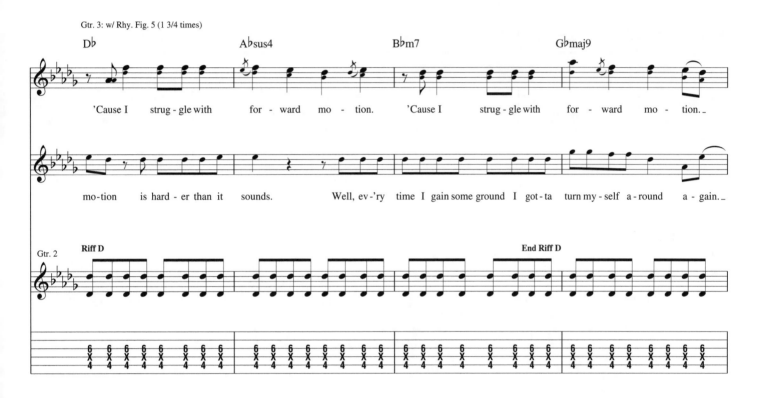

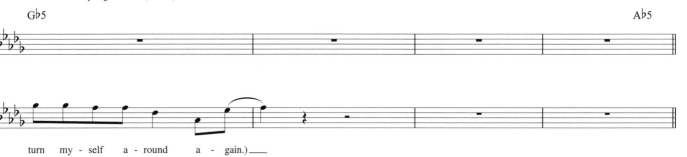

turn my - self a - round a - gain.) ____

Outro

Gtrs. 6 & 7: w/ Riffs C & C1 (3 3/4 times)

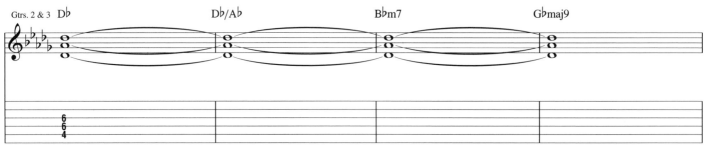

Gtrs. 2 & 3 tacet

'Cause I strug - gle with for - ward mo - tion. 'Cause I strug - gle with

for - ward mo - tion. We all strug - gle with for - ward mo - tion. ____

In Love With the 80's
(Pink Tux to the Prom)

Words and Music by Matt Thiessen

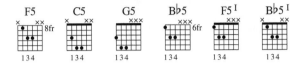

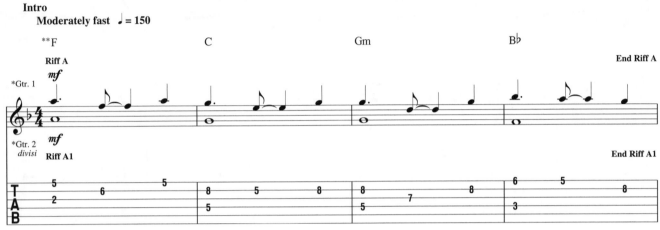

*Synth. arr. for gtr.

**Chord symbols reflect overall harmony.

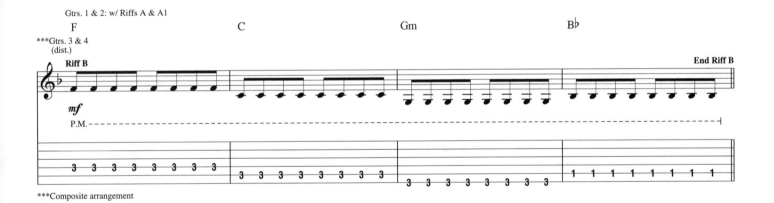

***Composite arrangement

Chorus

Gtrs. 3 & 4: w/ Rhy. Fig. 1
Gtr. 5: w/ Riff C

And I'm on-ly gon-na pierce my left ear, and I've been work-in' on this mus-tache all ___ sum-mer long, ___

___ and my fav-'rite band will al-ways be Tears For Fears, ___ and I'm gon-na wear a

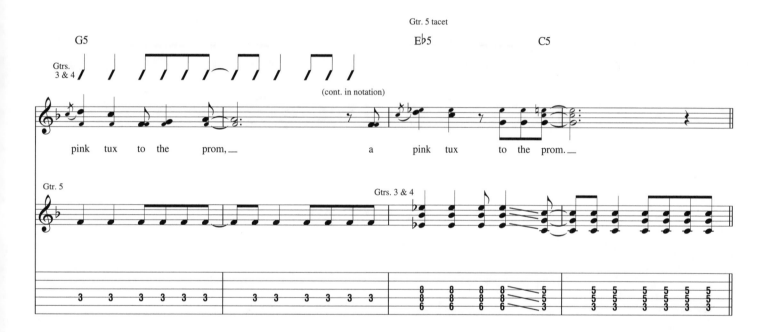

pink tux to the prom, ___ a pink tux to the prom. ___

Bridge

Gtrs. 3 & 4 tacet

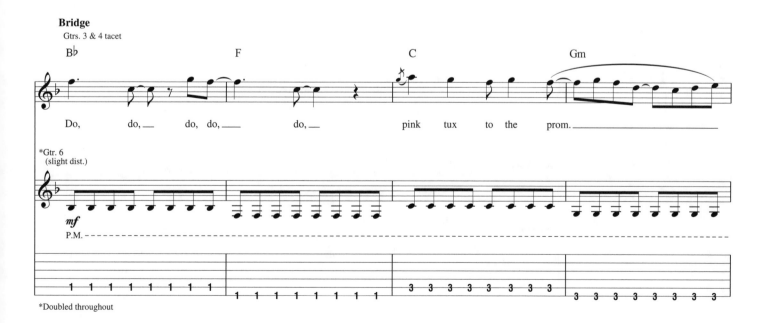

Do, do, ___ do, do, ___ do, ___ pink tux to the prom. _____

*Gtr. 6
(slight dist.)

*Doubled throughout

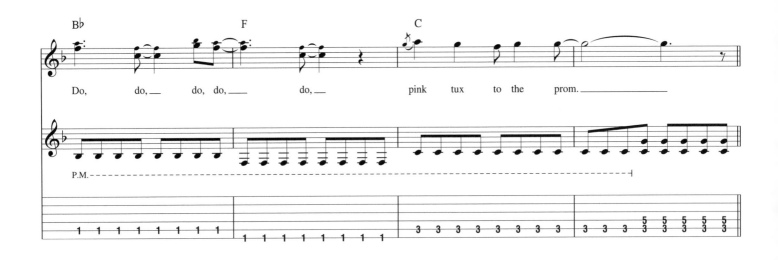

Do,   do,   do, do,   do,   pink tux to the prom.

P.M.

Chorus

Gtr. 6 tacet

F5   C5   G5   Bb5

Rhy. Fig. 2   End Rhy. Fig. 2

Gtrs.
3 & 4

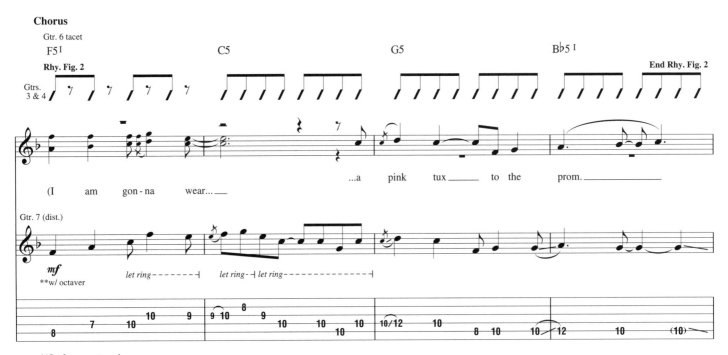

...a pink tux ___ to the prom.

(I am gon-na wear...___

Gtr. 7 (dist.)

mf
**w/ octaver

let ring   let ring - let ring

**Set for one octave above.

Gtrs. 3 & 4: w/ Rhy. Fig. 2

F5   C5   G5   Bb5

...what could pos - si - bly ___ go   wrong? ___

Live with - out a care,...) ___

Verse

3. When you're the pres - i - dent of the Break-fast Club, __ and you're not hes - i - tant to fall in love, __

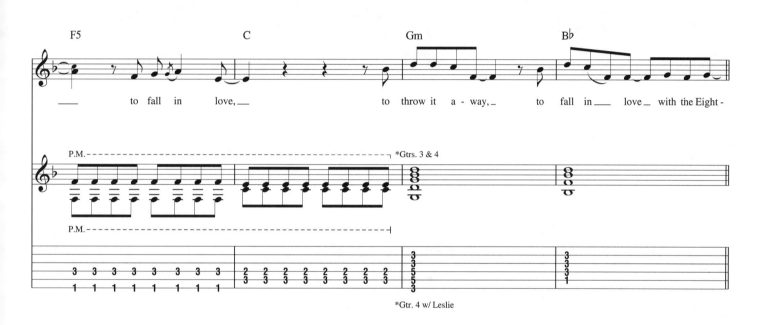

__ to fall in love, __ to throw it a - way, __ to fall in __ love __ with the Eight-

*Gtr. 4 w/ Leslie

Interlude

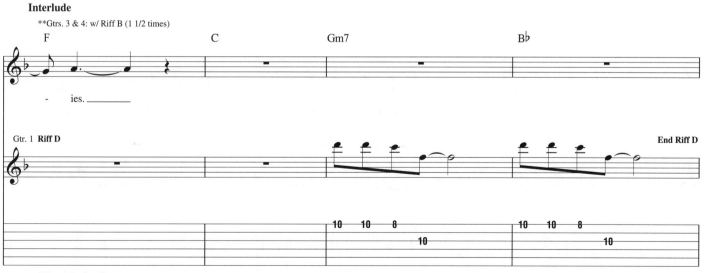

- ies. _____

**Gtr. 4; Leslie off

Outro

Gtrs. 1 & 2: w/ Riffs A & A1 (6 times)
Gtrs. 3 & 4: w/ Riff B (6 times)
Gtrs. 5 & 7 tacet

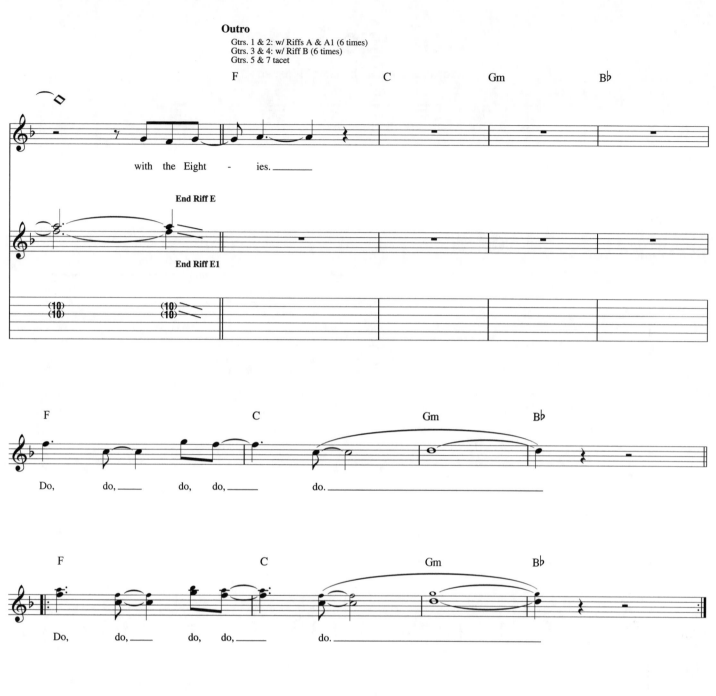

with the Eight - ies. _____

End Riff E

End Riff E1

Do, do, ____ do, do, ____ do. _____

Do, do, ____ do, do, ____ do. _____

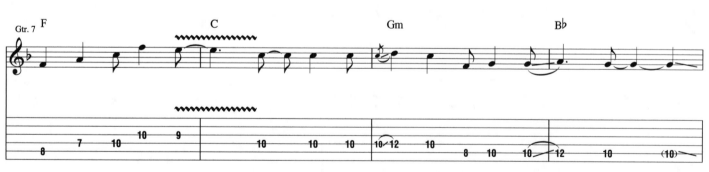

Gtr. 7

Gtrs. 5 & 7: w/ Riffs E & E1

Begin fade

Fade out

College Kids

Words and Music by Matt Thiessen

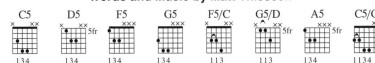

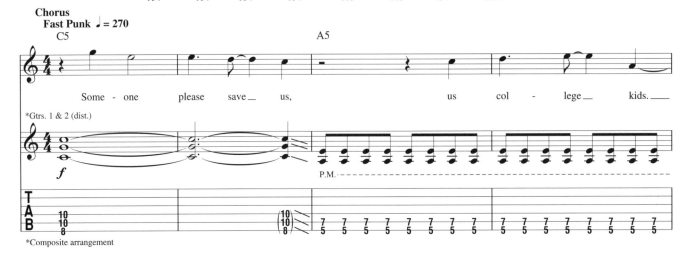

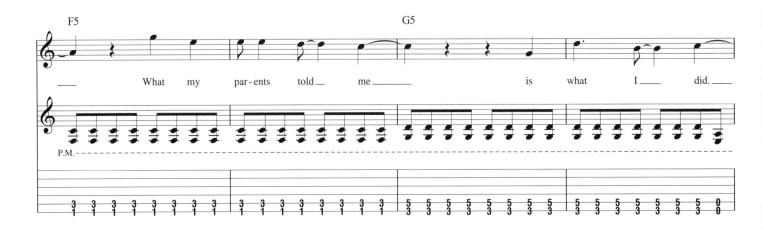

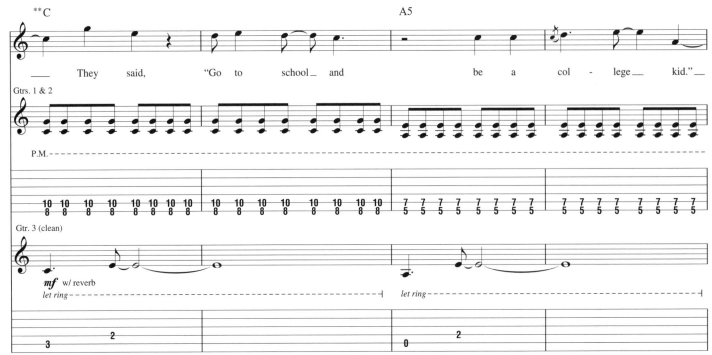

*Composite arrangement

**Chord symbols reflect overall harmony.

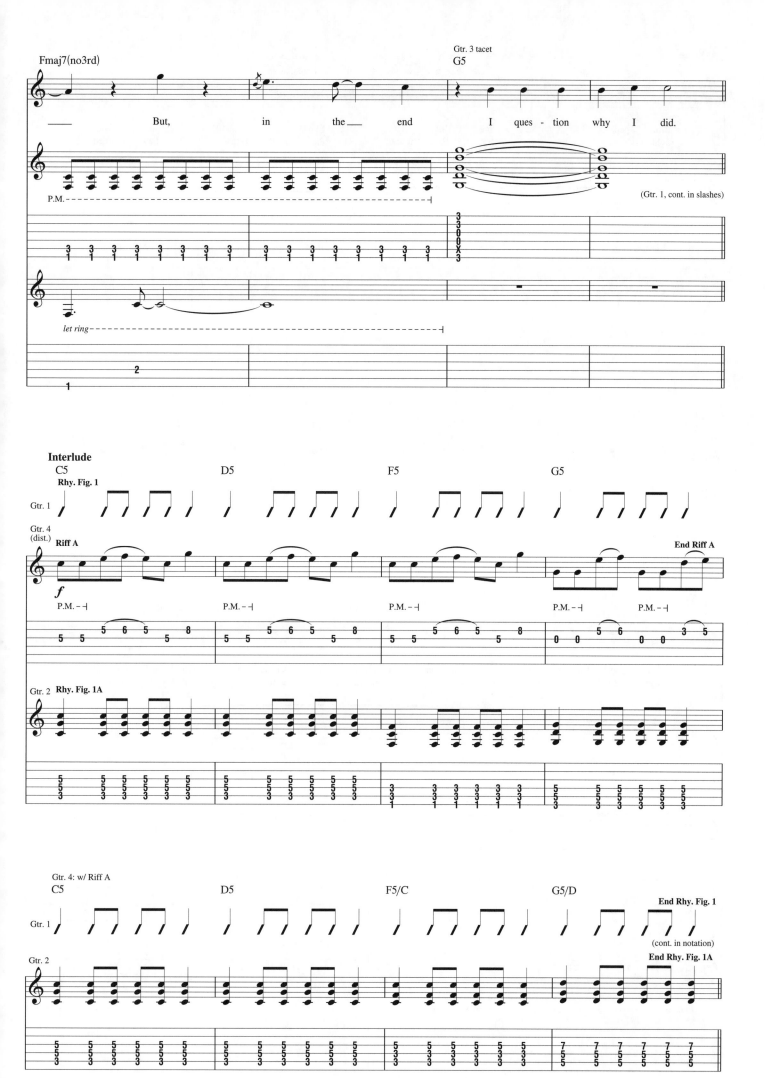

%%% Verse

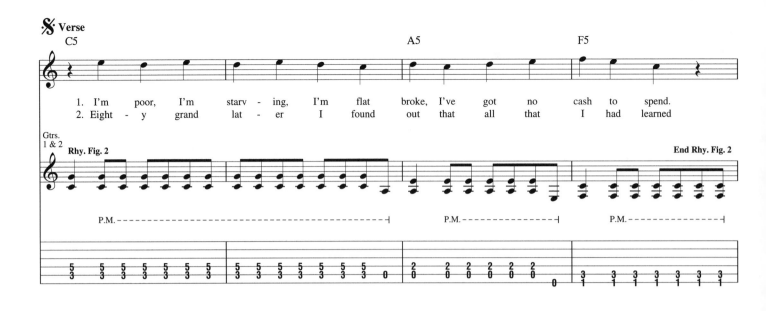

1. I'm poor, I'm starv - ing, I'm flat broke, I've got no cash to spend.
2. Eight - y grand lat - er I found out that all that I had learned

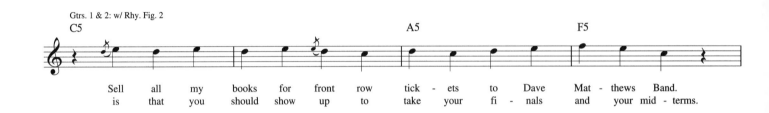

Sell all my books for front row tick - ets to Dave Mat - thews Band.
is that you should show up to take your fi - nals and your mid - terms.

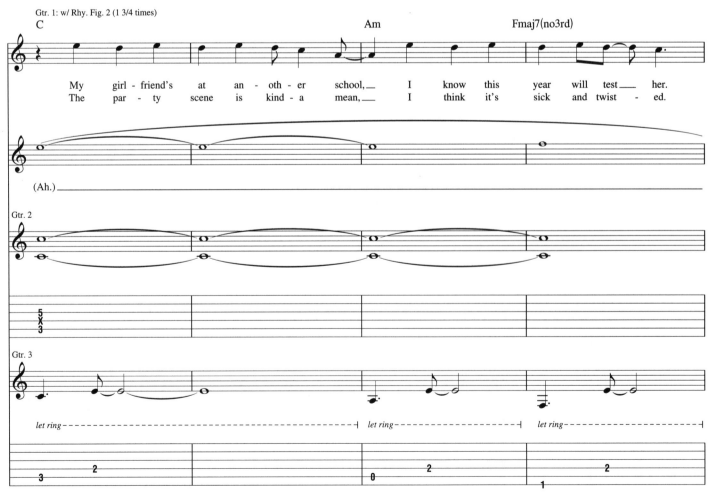

My girl - friend's at an - oth - er school,__ I know this year will test__ her.
The par - ty scene is kind - a mean,__ I think it's sick and twist - ed.

I called, found out she had three oth-er boy-friends last se-mes-
The Na-vy showed up at my door, they claimed that I en-list-

- ter. _____
- ed. _____

And that's why ___ I say...

(Oh,

𝄋𝄋 Chorus

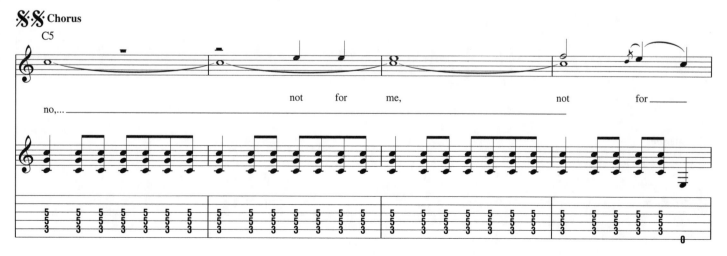

not for me, not for ___

no,...

me. Call it tor - ture, call it u - ni - ver - si - ty.

...arts and crafts is all I _____
No,...) _____

To Coda 1 ⊕
To Coda 2 ⊕

need. I'll take cal - lig - ra - phy and then I'll make a fake de - gree.___

D.S. al Coda 1

Interlude

Gtrs. 1 & 2: w/ Rhy. Figs. 1 & 1A
Gtr. 4: w/ Riff A (2 times)

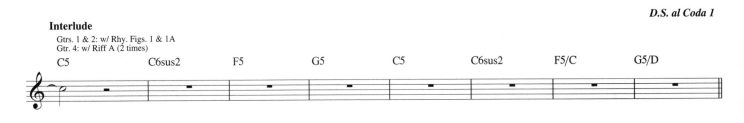

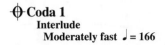

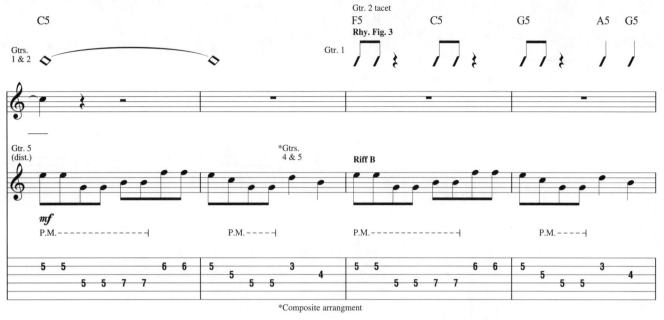

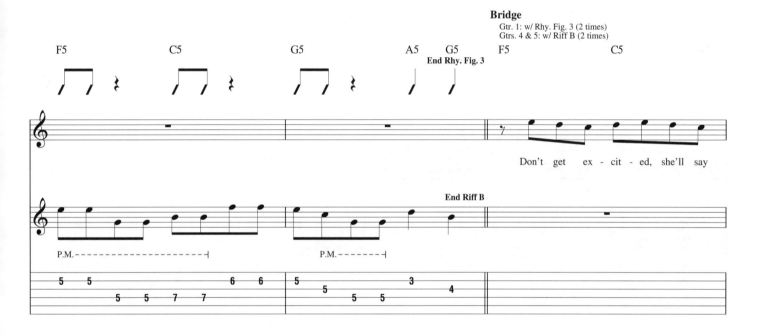

*Composite arrangement

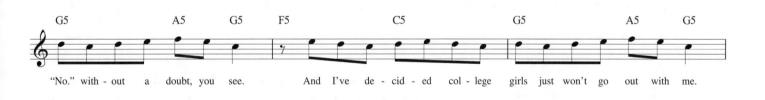

Don't get ex - cit - ed, she'll say

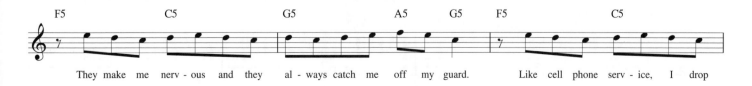

"No." with - out a doubt, you see. And I've de - cid - ed col - lege girls just won't go out with me.

They make me nerv - ous and they al - ways catch me off my guard. Like cell phone serv - ice, I drop

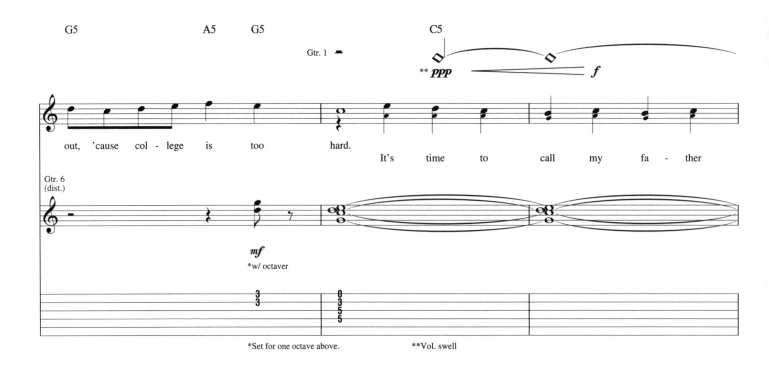

*Set for one octave above. **Vol. swell

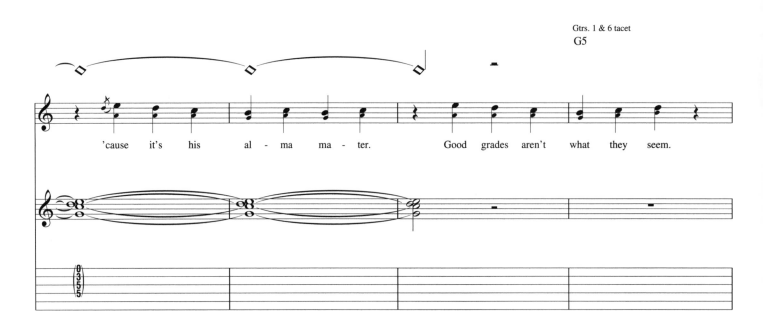

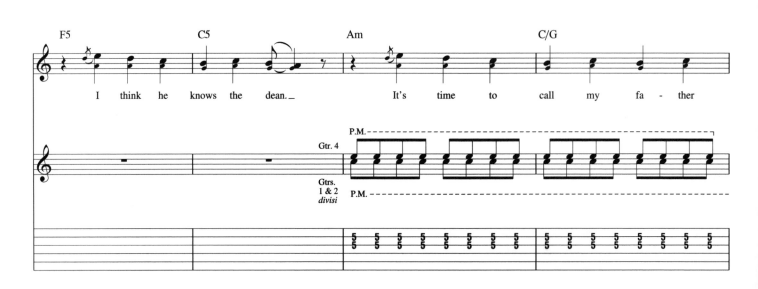

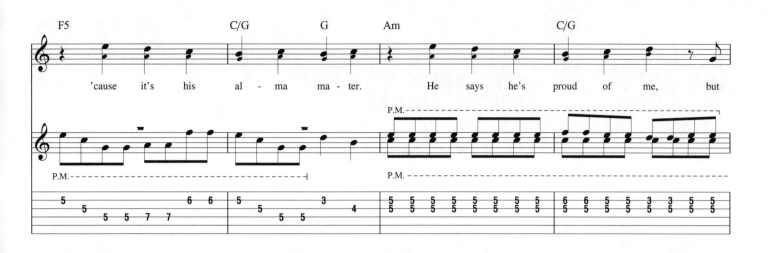

Interlude
A tempo

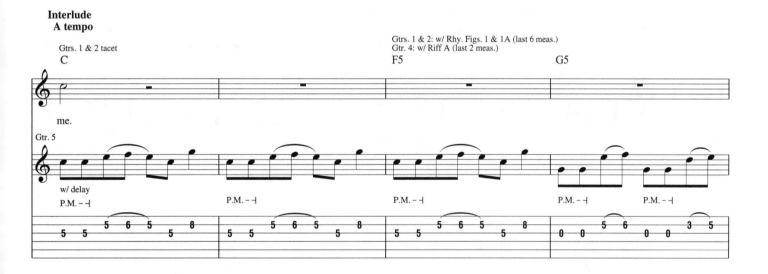

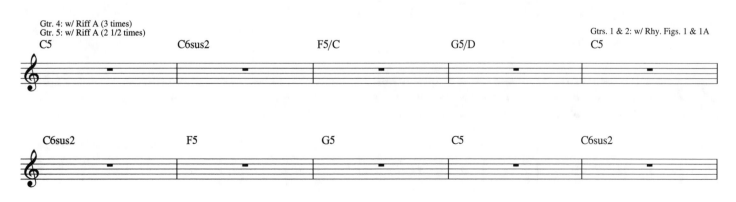

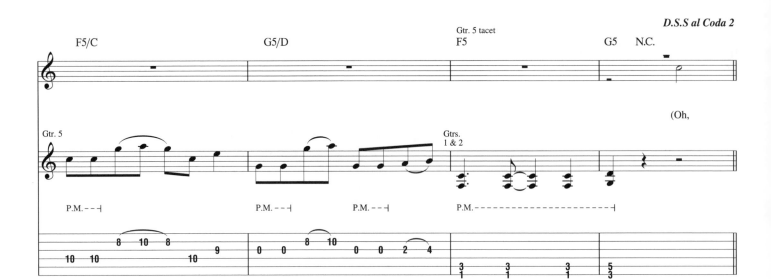

Coda 2
Chorus

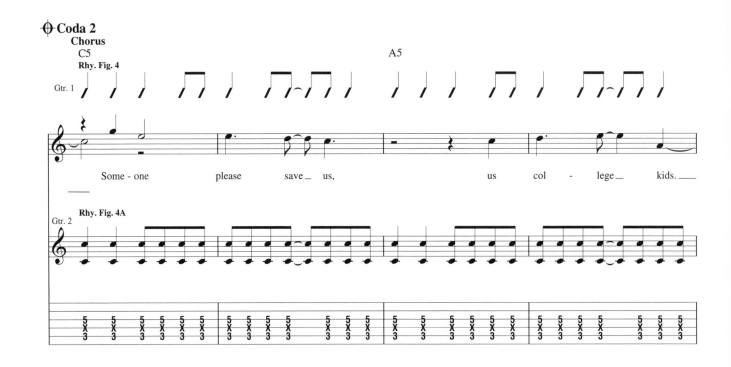

Some - one please save_ us, us col - lege_ kids.__

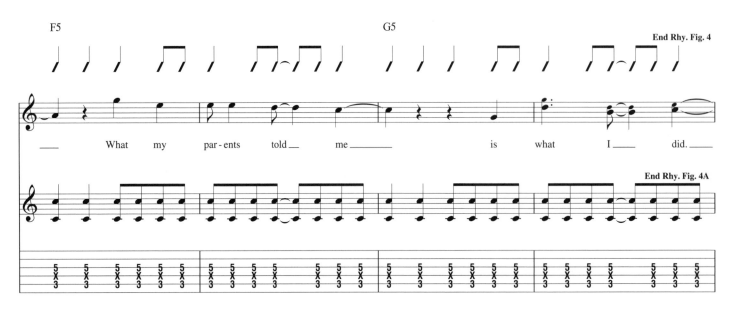

__ What my par - ents told __ me _____ is what I ____ did. _____

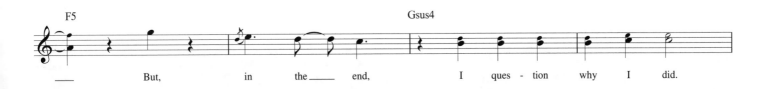

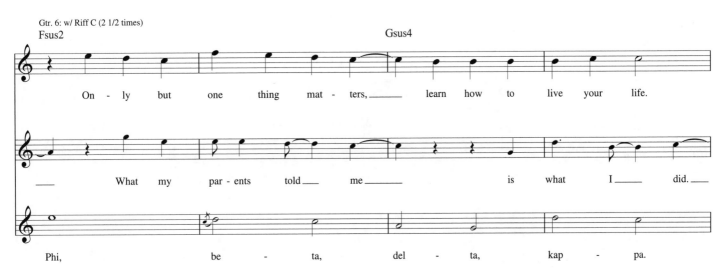

Do what will make God hap - py, _____ do what you feel is right.

_____ They said, "Go to school ___ and be a col - lege ___ kid." ___

Phi, be - ta, del - ta, kap - pa.) _____

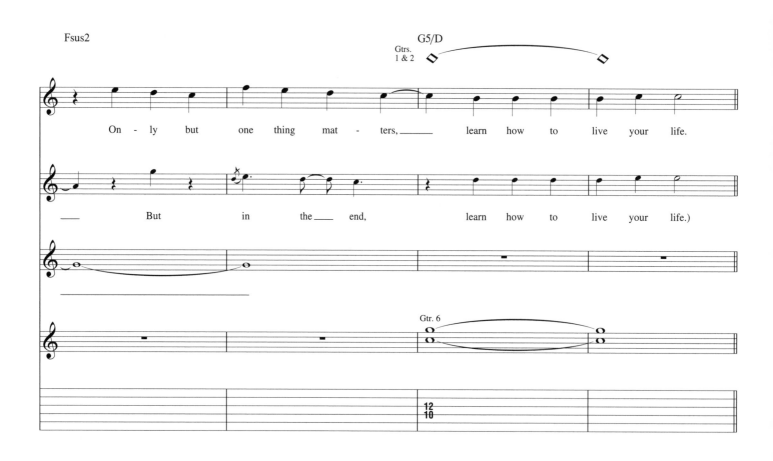

On - ly but one thing mat - ters, _____ learn how to live your life.

_____ But in the ___ end, learn how to live your life.)

Outro

Free time

Segue to "Trademark"

Gtr. 6 tacet

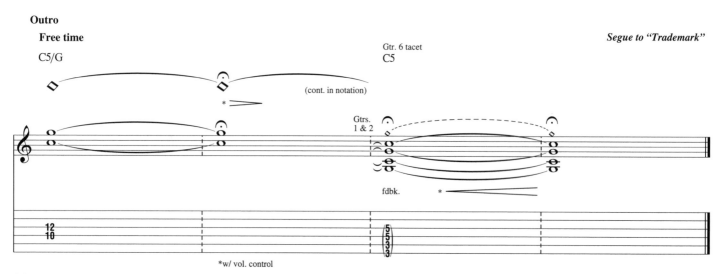

(cont. in notation)

*w/ vol. control

Trademark

Words and Music by Matt Thiessen

Drop D tuning:
(low to high) D-A-D-G-B-E

Intro
Moderately fast ♩ = 179

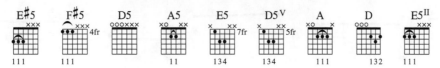

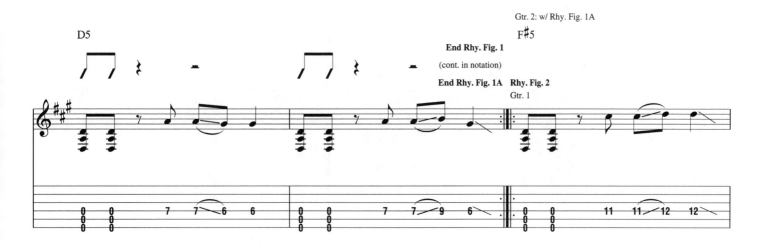

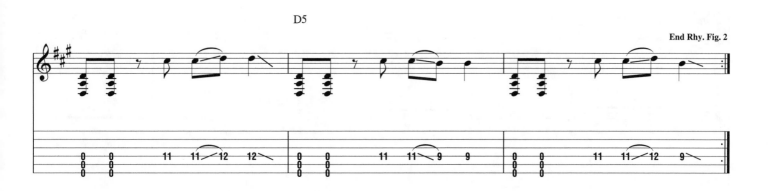

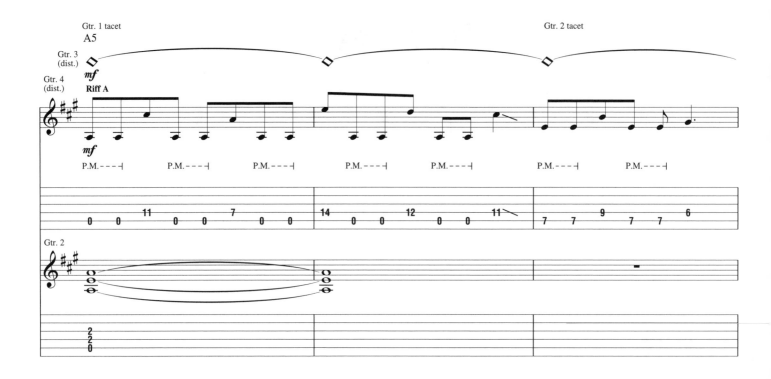

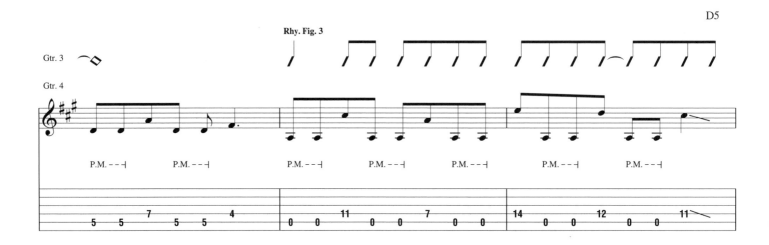

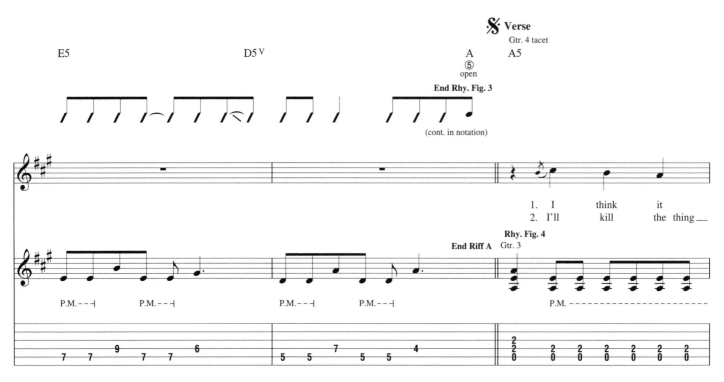

might just be___ al - right / to leave what mat - ters out___ of sight.
___ that turns me a - way, / am - pu - tate the arm___ that will dis - o - bey,

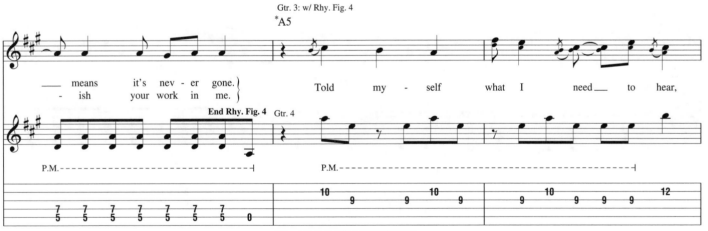

Old hab - its die hard, hold - ing on. / In - ev - i - ta - ble___
with - draw from ev - 'ry - thing that's hurt - ing me / un - til you fin -

Gtr. 3: w/ Rhy. Fig. 4

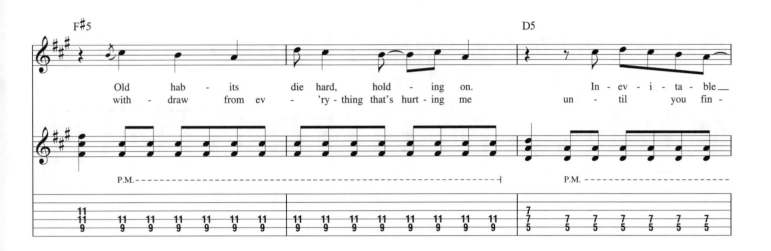

___ means it's nev - er gone.} / Told my - self what I need___ to hear,
- ish your work in me.}

End Rhy. Fig. 4   Gtr. 4

*Chord symbols reflect overall harmony.

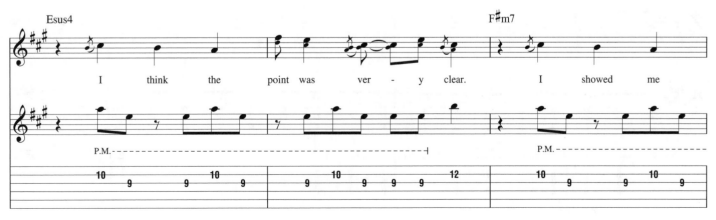

I think the point was ver - y clear. / I showed me

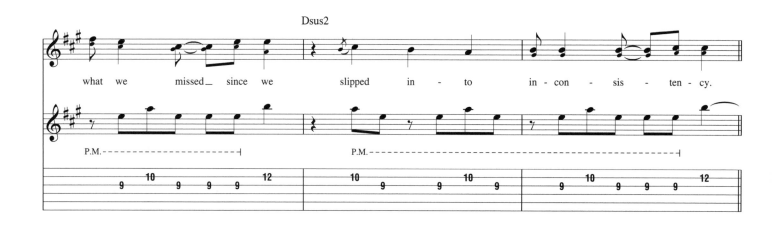

what we missed___ since we slipped in - to in - con - sis - ten - cy.

Pre-Chorus

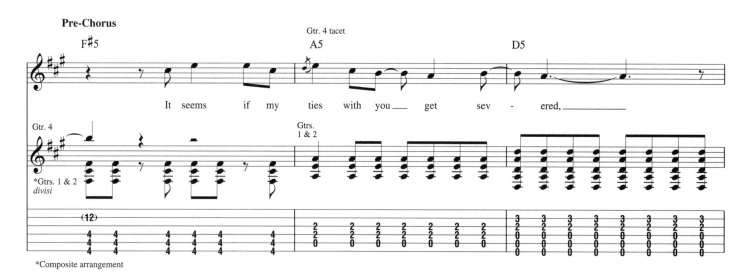

It seems if my ties with you___ get sev - ered,_____

*Composite arrangement

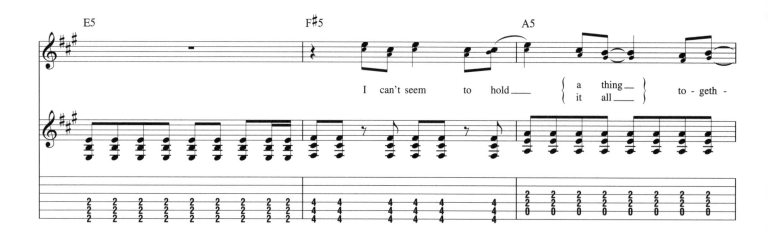

I can't seem to hold___ { a thing___ } { it all___ } to - geth -

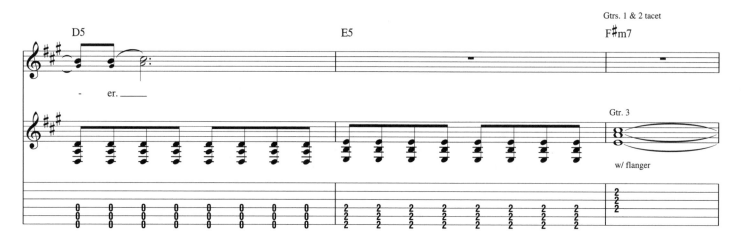

- er.___

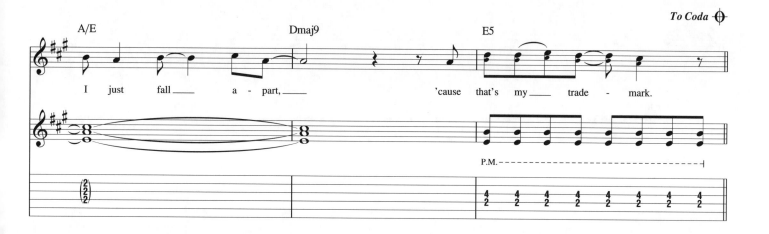

Chorus

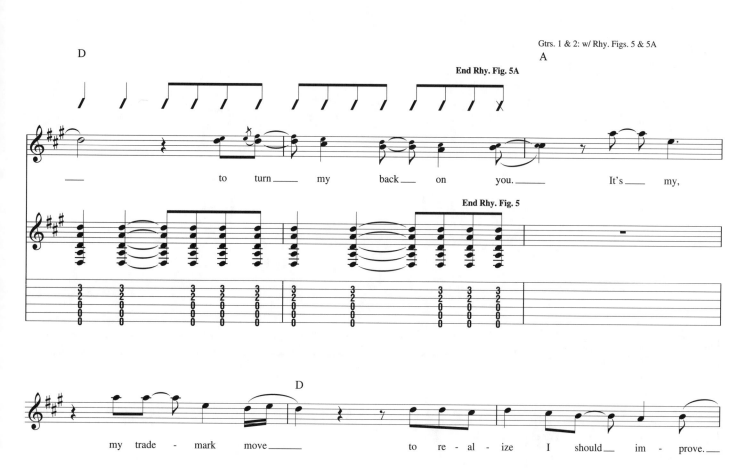

Interlude
Gtr. 1: w/ Rhy. Fig. 1

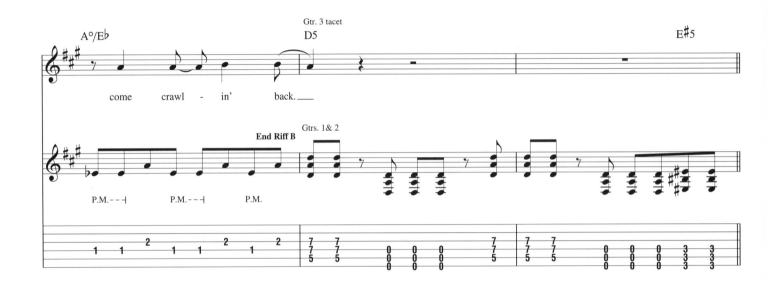

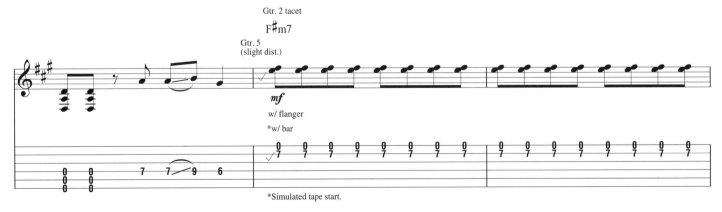

*Simulated tape start.

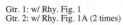

Gtr. 1: w/ Rhy. Fig. 1
Gtr. 2: w/ Rhy. Fig. 1A (2 times)

Gtr. 1: w/ Rhy. Fig. 2

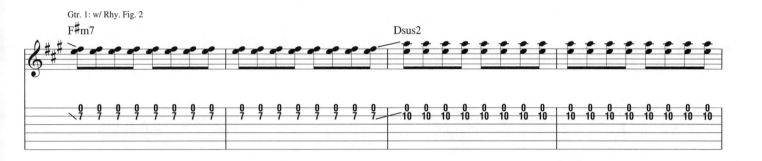

Gtr. 3: w/ Rhy. Fig. 3 (2 times)
Gtr. 4: w/ Riff A
Gtr. 5 tacet

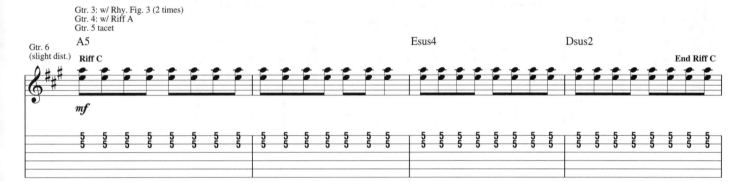

D.S. al Coda

⊕ Coda

Chorus

Gtr. 1: w/ Rhy. Fig. 5 (2 times)

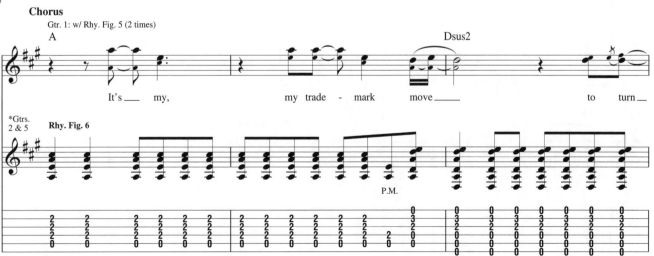

It's ___ my,   my trade - mark   move ___   to turn ___

*Composite arrangement

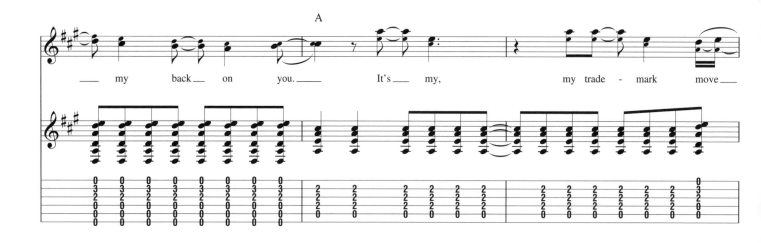

my back on you. It's my, my trade - mark move

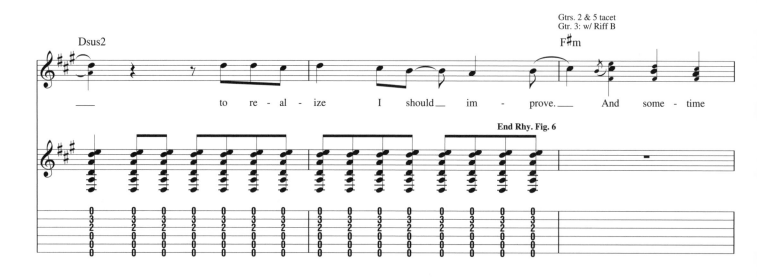

to re - al - ize I should im - prove. And some - time

soon af - ter that you'll see me come crawl - in' back.

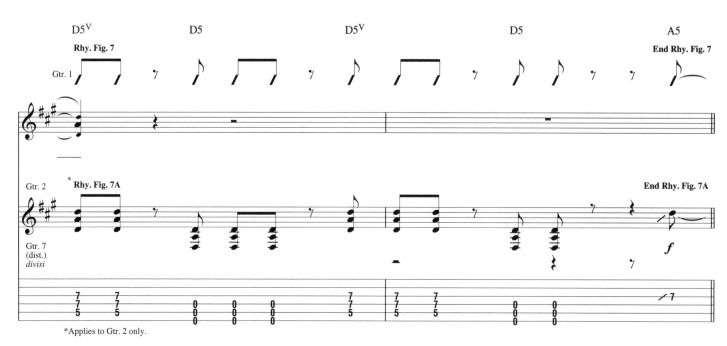

*Applies to Gtr. 2 only.

Interlude
Gtr. 2 tacet

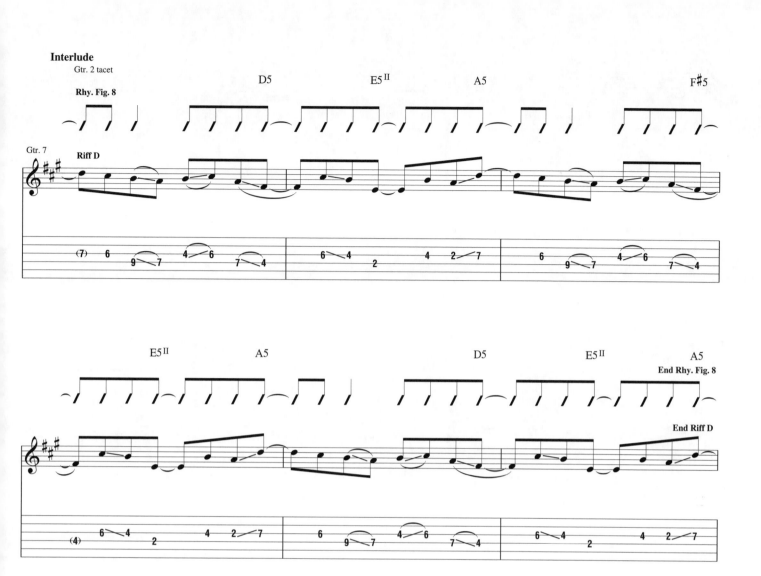

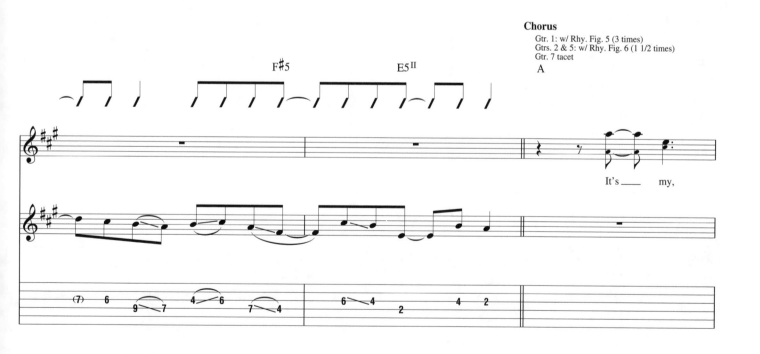

Chorus
Gtr. 1: w/ Rhy. Fig. 5 (3 times)
Gtrs. 2 & 5: w/ Rhy. Fig. 6 (1 1/2 times)
Gtr. 7 tacet

It's ___ my, my trade - mark move ___ to re - al -

ize I should ___ im - prove. ___ It's ___ my, my trade - mark move ___

___ to turn ___ my back ___ on you. ___ It's ___ my,

Gtrs
2 & 5

Gtr. 1

Gtrs. 1 & 5 tacet

Gtr. 2

(cont. in notation)

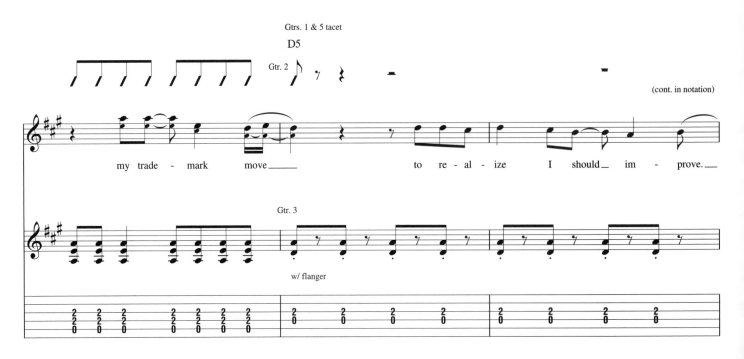

my trade - mark move ___ to re - al - ize I should ___ im - prove. ___

Gtr. 3

w/ flanger

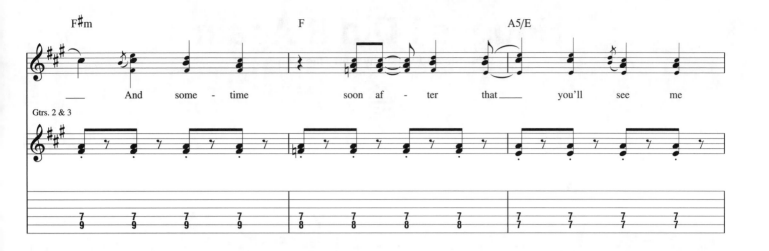

Gtrs. 1 & 2: w/ Rhy. Figs. 7 & 7A
Gtr. 3 tacet

w/ wah-wah

Outro

Gtr. 1: w/ Rhy. Fig. 8
Gtr. 7: w/ Riff D

Segue to "Hoopes I Did It Again"

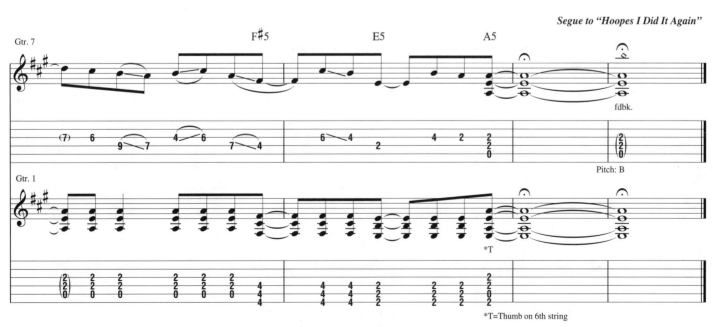

*T=Thumb on 6th string

Hoopes I Did It Again

Words and Music by Matt Thiessen

A5

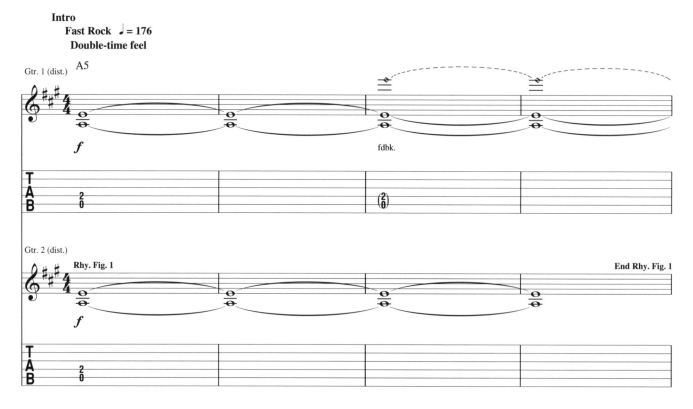

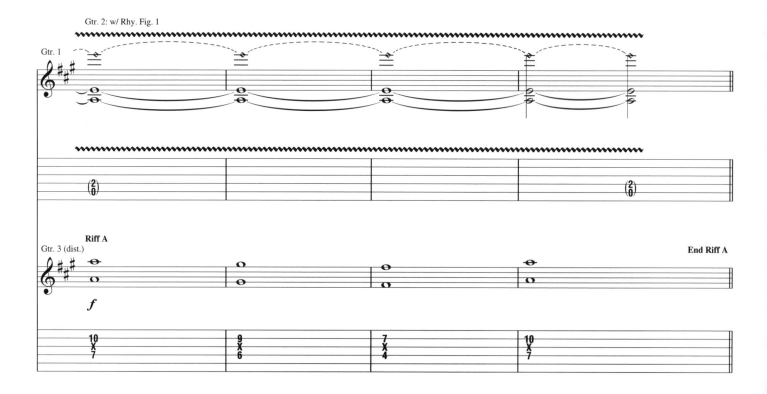

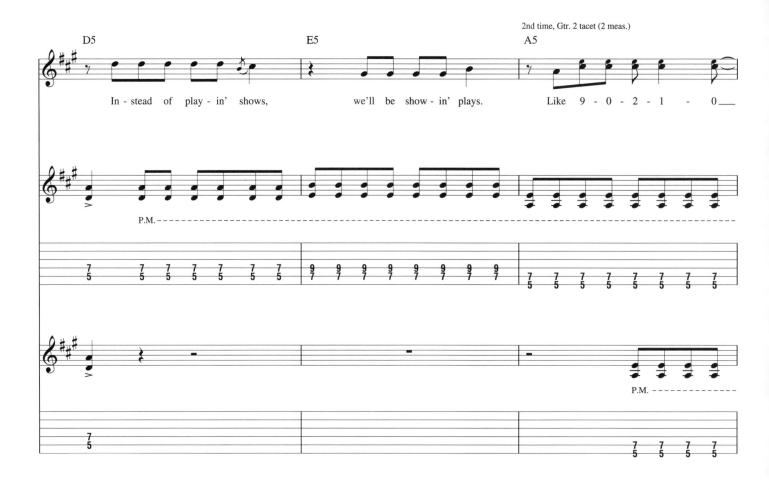

2nd time, Gtr. 2 tacet (2 meas.)

In - stead of play - in' shows, we'll be show - in' plays. Like 9 - 0 - 2 - 1 - 0

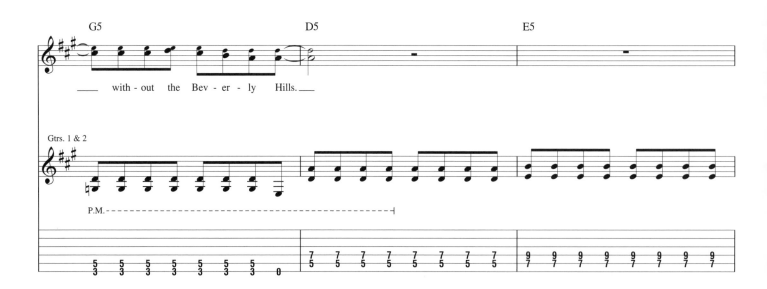

___ with - out the Bev - er - ly Hills. ___

74

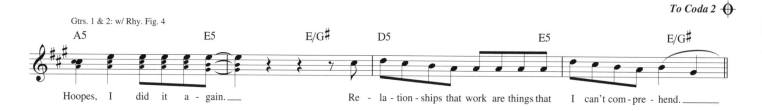

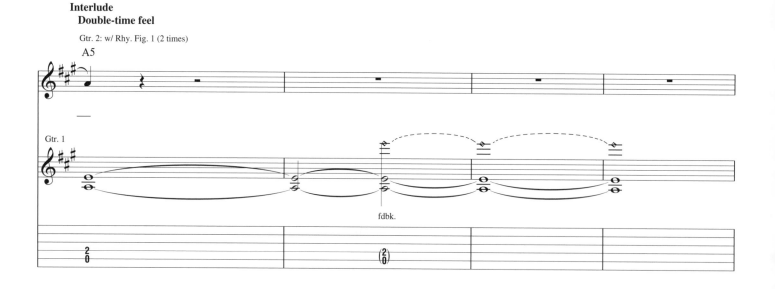

✛ Coda 1

Double-time feel

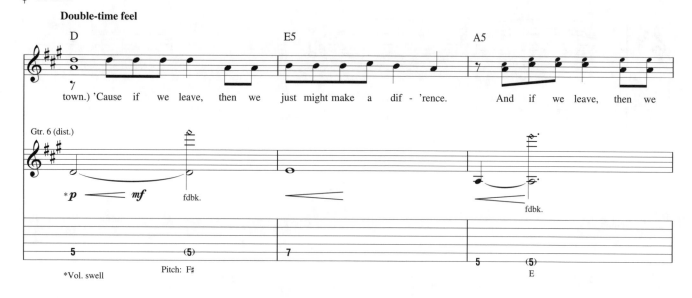

*Vol. swell

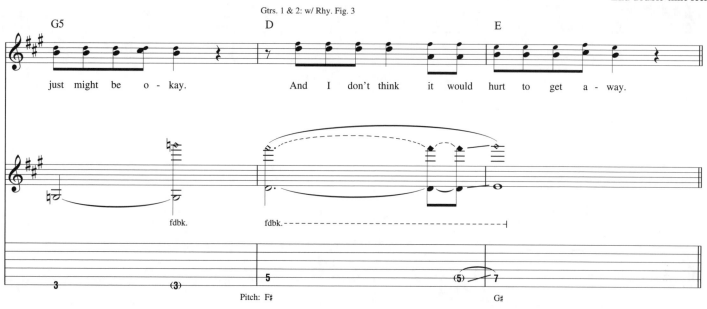

D.S.S. al Coda 2
End double-time feel

✛ Coda 2

Interlude

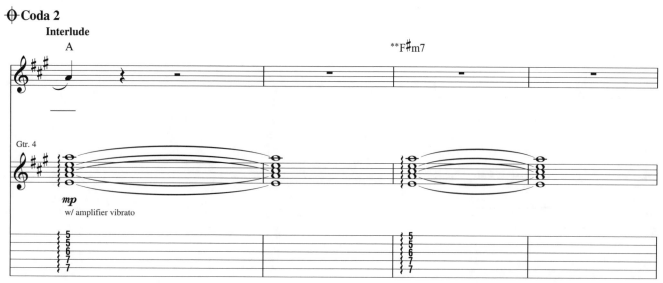

**Chord symbols reflect overall harmony.

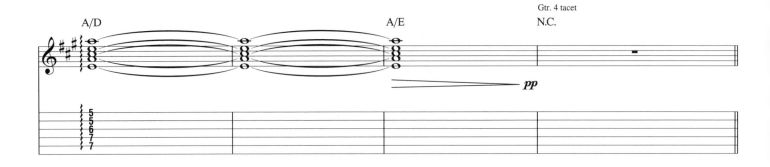

Bridge

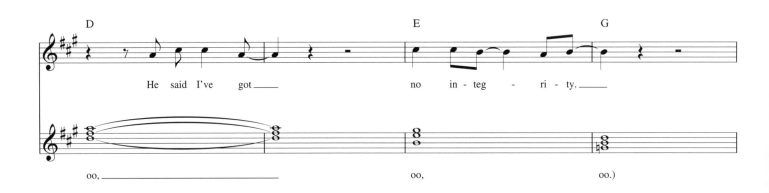

Dan Ba - ki - tus said I'm shal - low.

(Oo, _____ oo, _____

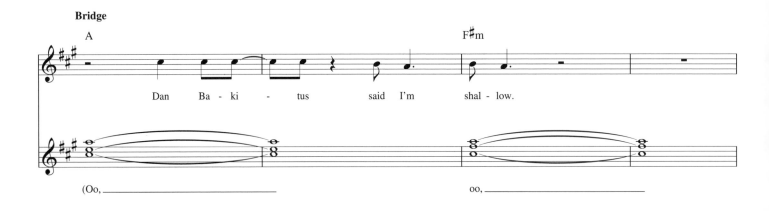

He said I've got _____ no in - teg - ri - ty. _____

oo, _____ oo, oo.)

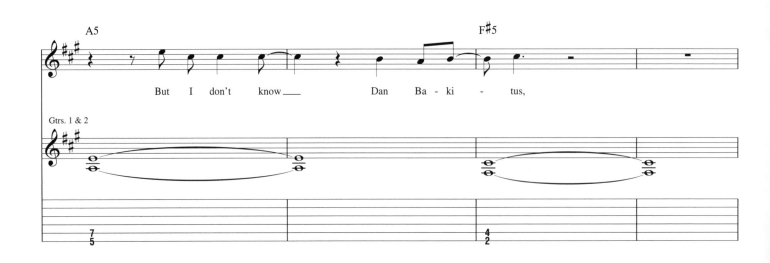

But I don't know _____ Dan Ba - ki - tus,

Gtrs. 1 & 2

Overthinking

Words and Music by Matt Thiessen

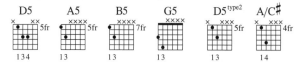

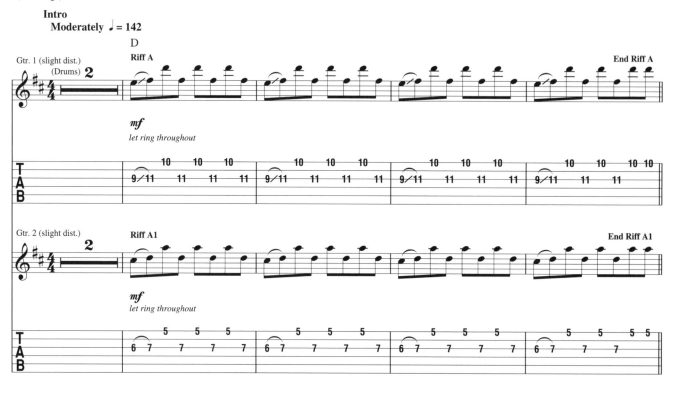

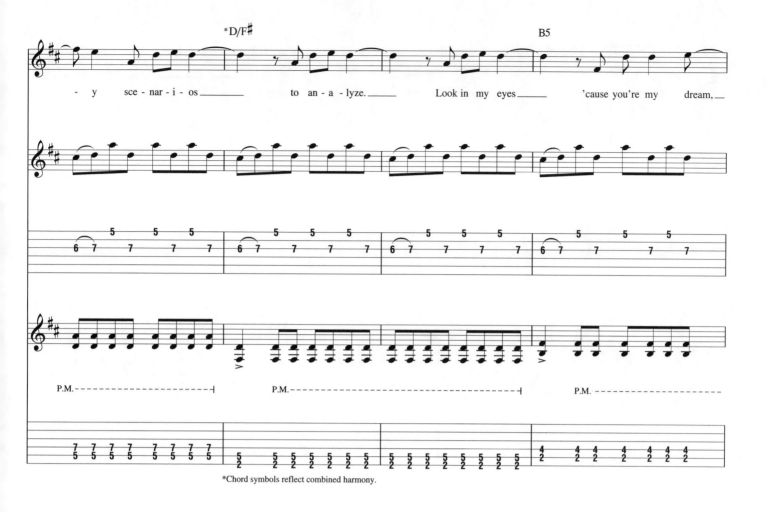

*Chord symbols reflect combined harmony.

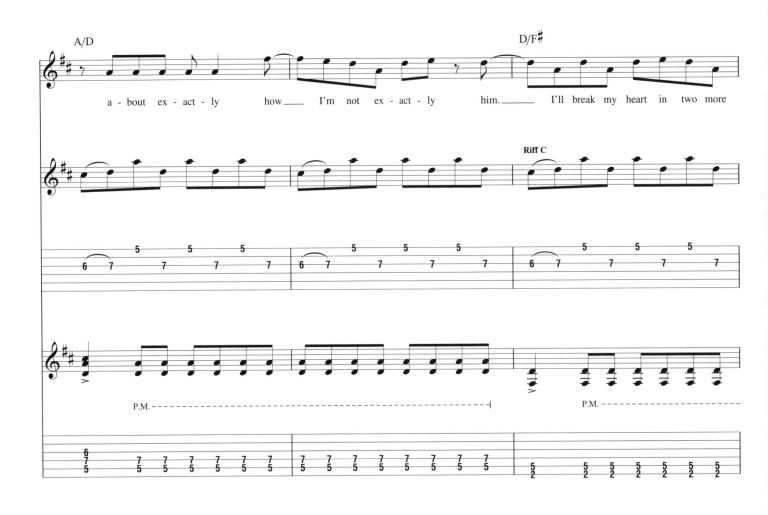

a - bout ex - act - ly   how___   I'm not ex - act - ly   him.___   I'll break my heart in two more

times than you could ev - er do   'cause you're my   dream,___   please   come___   true.

Gtrs. 3 & 4: w/ Rhy. Figs. 3 & 3A

B5   G5   D5   A/C#

fore.   And   if   there's   one ____ in this world, ___ you let me know ___ you're not ___ that

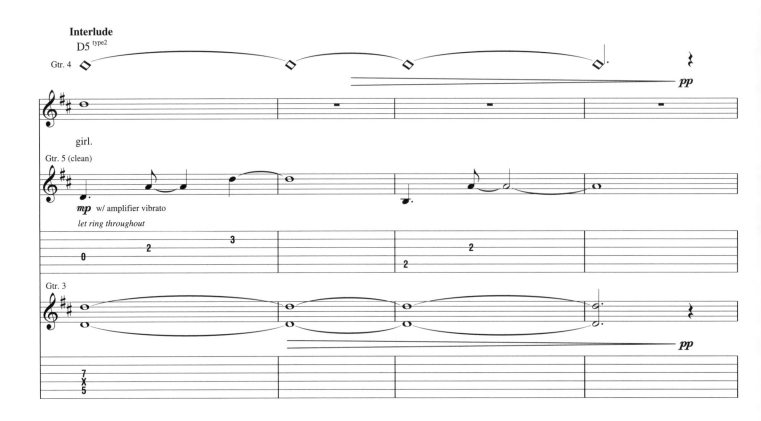

Interlude

D5 type2

Gtr. 4

girl.

Gtr. 5 (clean)

mp   w/ amplifier vibrato

let ring throughout

Gtr. 3

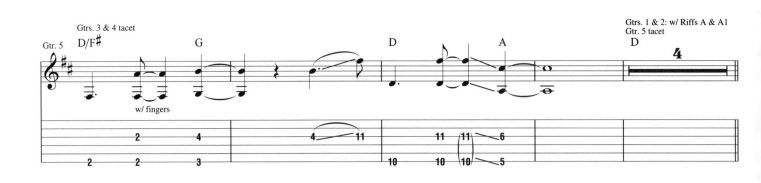

Gtrs. 3 & 4 tacet

Gtrs. 1 & 2: w/ Riffs A & A1
Gtr. 5 tacet

Gtr. 5   D/F#   G   D   A   D

w/ fingers

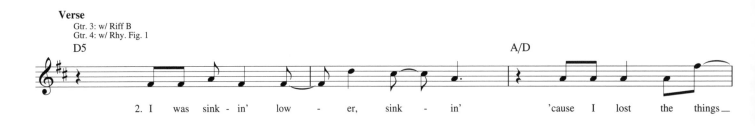

Verse

Gtr. 3: w/ Riff B
Gtr. 4: w/ Rhy. Fig. 1

D5   A/D

2. I   was   sink - in'   low - er,   sink - in'   'cause I lost the things ___

D/F#

___ I   held ___ on   to. ___ They let me think a thought, a thought that I would know was not

of see-in' my ___ dream come ___ true. I was think-in', ov-

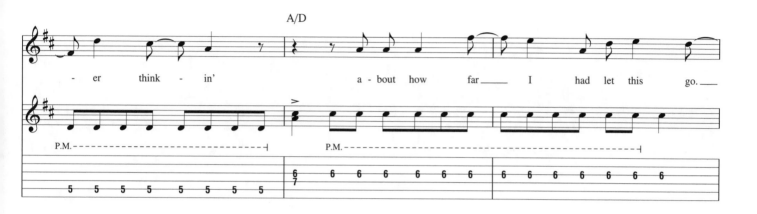

-er think - in' a - bout how far ___ I had let this go. ___

Gtr. 3: w/ Riff C

___ One more guy girl cli - ché, I know now you're just in the way of me and my ___

Pre-Chorus
Gtr. 3: w/ Riff D
Gtr. 4: w/ Rhy. Fig. 2 (1st 4 meas.)

___ dream come ___ true. 'Cause I think way ___ too much ___

𝄋𝄋
Gtr. 3: w/ Riff E (1st 2 meas., 4 times)

on a one ___ track mind, _____ and

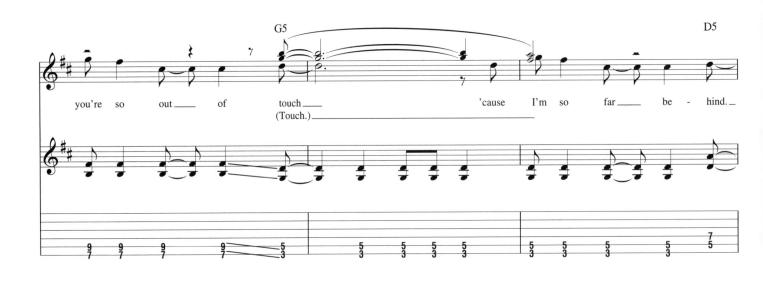

you're so out of touch 'cause I'm so far be - hind.
(Touch.)

Gtr. 4: w/ Rhy. Fig. 2

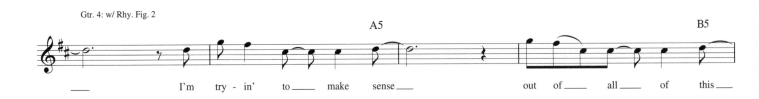

I'm try - in' to make sense out of all of this

To Coda 2
D.S. al Coda 1

Gtr. 3: w/ Riff E

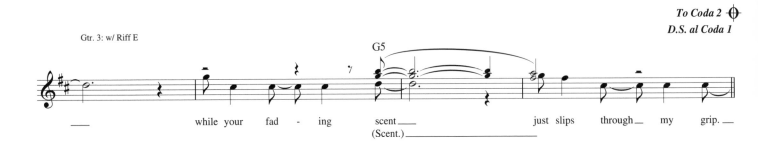

while your fad - ing scent just slips through my grip.
(Scent.)

Coda 1
Interlude

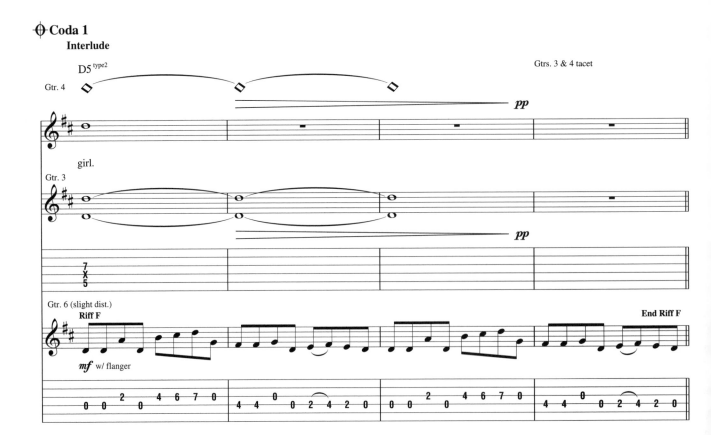

girl.

Gtr. 6 (slight dist.)
Riff F   End Riff F

mf w/ flanger

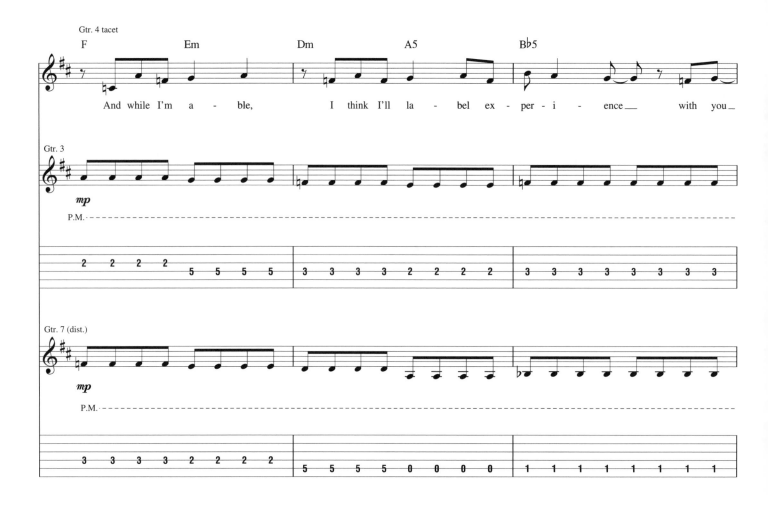

⊕ Coda 2

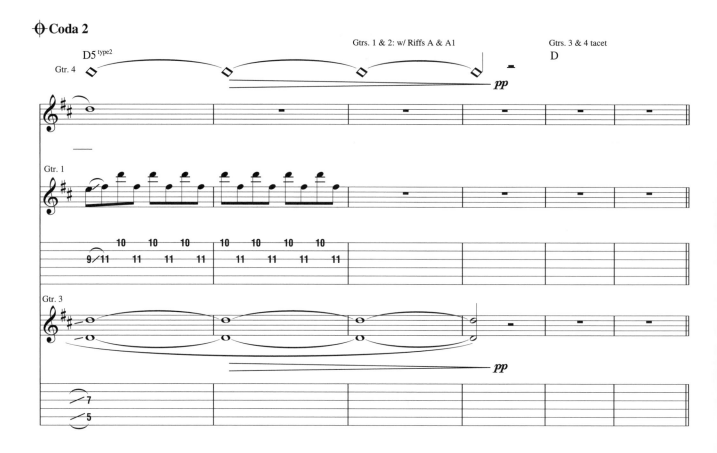

Outro-Verse

Gtr. 3: w/ Riff B (1st 7 meas.)
Gtr. 4: w/ Rhy. Fig. 1 (1st 7 meas.)

I was think - in', ov - er think - in' 'cause there's just too man - y sce - nar - i - os

to think a - bout, to fig - ure out. If you're my dream, please come true.

I Am Understood

Words and Music by Matt Thiessen

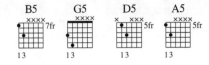

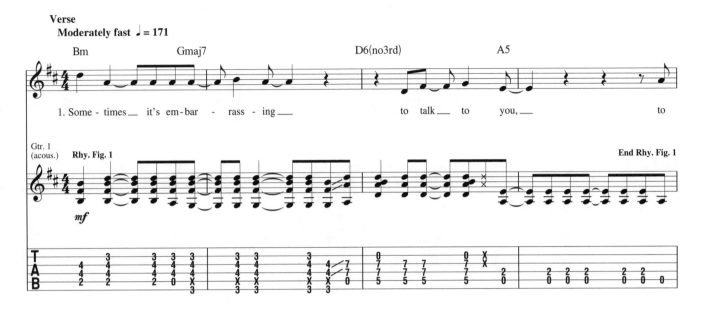

you re-cite my words right____ back to me. Be-fore I____ e-ven

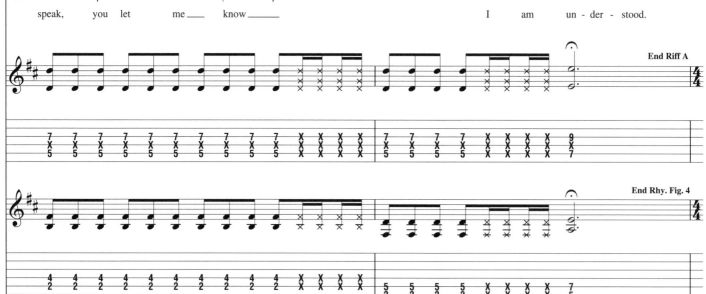

speak, you let me____ know____ I am un-der-stood.

End Riff A

End Rhy. Fig. 4

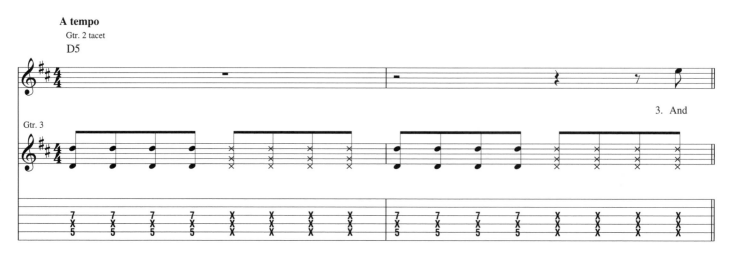

A tempo

Gtr. 2 tacet

D5

3. And

Gtr. 3

94

Verse

Gtrs. 2 & 3: w/ Rhy. Figs. 2 & 2A (3 1/2 times)

some - times___ I spend___ my time___ just try - ing to___ es - cape.___ I

work so hard,___ so des - p'rate - ly___ in an at - tempt to cre - ate space___

'cause I___ want dis - tance from the ut - most im - por - tant thing___ I know.___

___ I see your love,___ then turn my back___ and

Gtr. 2: w/ Rhy. Fig. 3

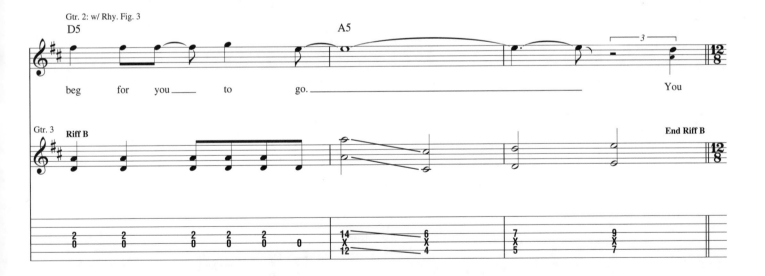

beg for you___ to go.___ You

Chorus

Gtr. 2: w/ Rhy. Fig. 4
Gtr. 3: w/ Riff A

looked in - to my life and___ nev - er stopped and you're think - in'___ all my

thoughts are so sim - ple, but so beau - ti - ful.___ And

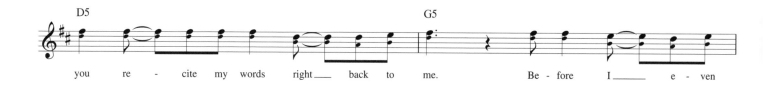

you re - cite my words right___ back to me. Be - fore I___ e - ven

speak, you let me___ know___ I am un - der - stood.

Interlude
Slower ♩ = 120

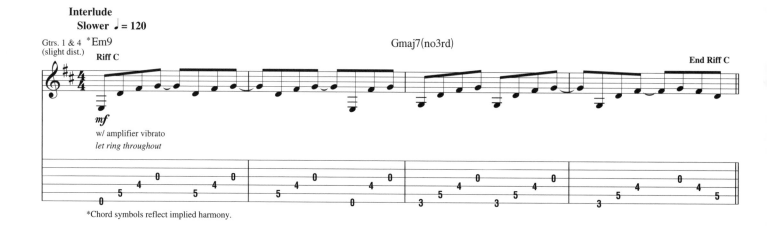

*Chord symbols reflect implied harmony.

Bridge

Gtrs. 1 & 4: w/ Riff C (1 1/2 times)

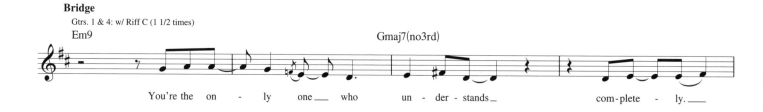

You're the on - ly one___ who un - der - stands___ com - plete - ly.___

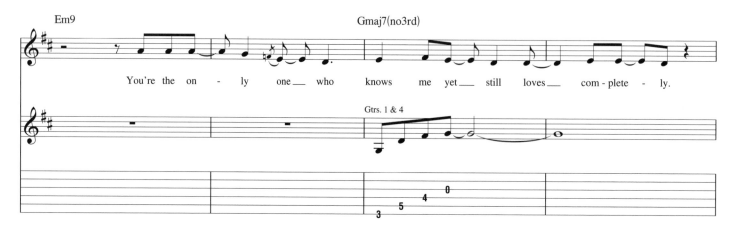

You're the on - ly one___ who knows me yet___ still loves___ com - plete - ly.

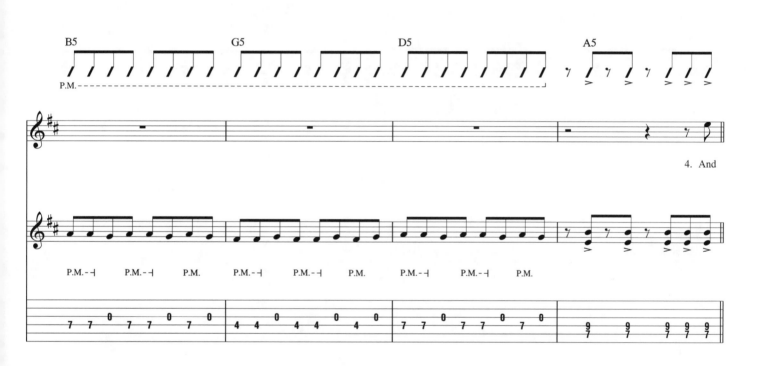

4. And

Verse

some - times____ the place____ I'm at____ is at a loss____ for words.____

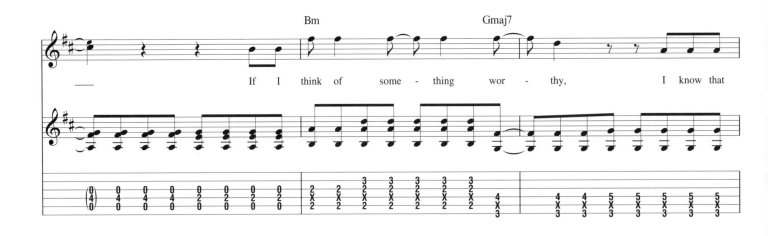

If I think of some - thing wor - thy, I know that

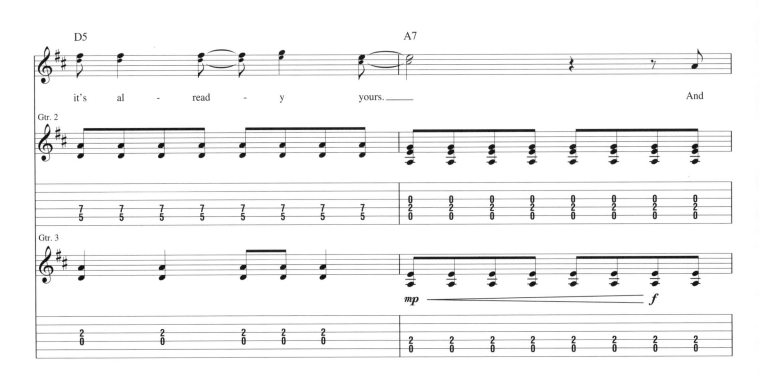

it's al - read - y yours.____ And

through the times__ I've fad - ed and __ you've out - lined me __ a - gain,__ you've

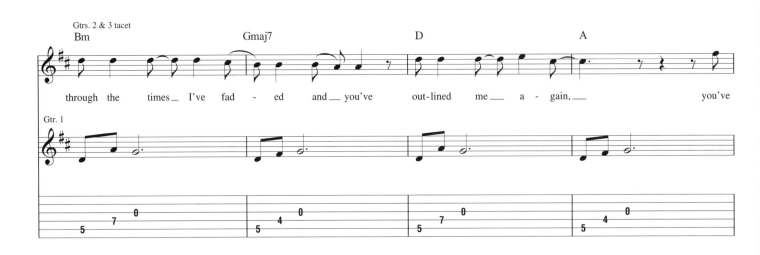

just pa - tient - ly wait - ed to bring me back__ and then____ you

⊕ **Coda**

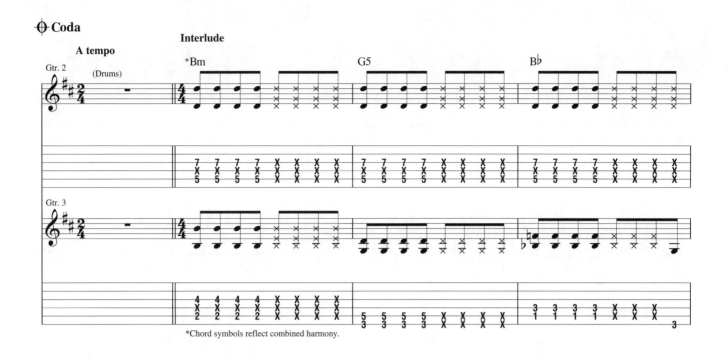

*Chord symbols reflect combined harmony.

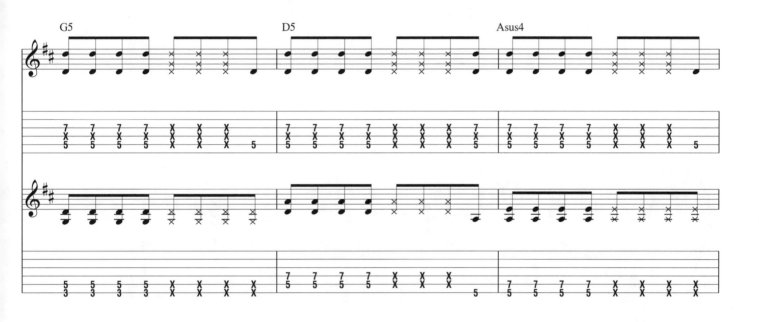

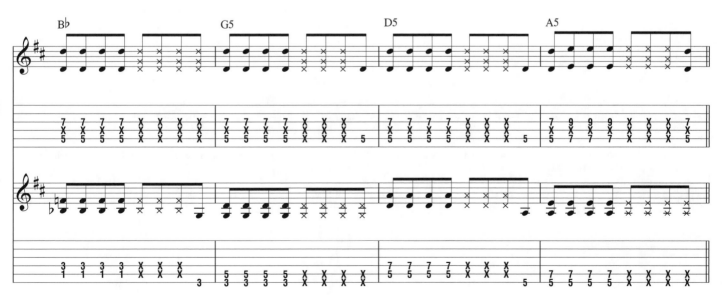

Outro

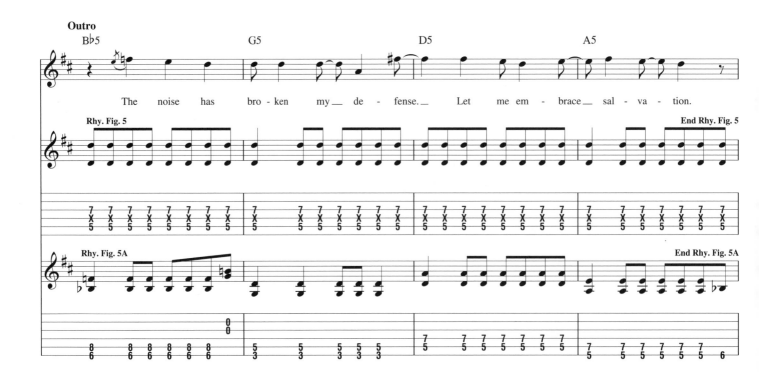

Gtrs. 2 & 3: w/ Rhy. Fig. 5 & 5A (6 times)

Your voice has bro - ken my __ de - fense. __ Let me em - brace __ sal - va - tion.

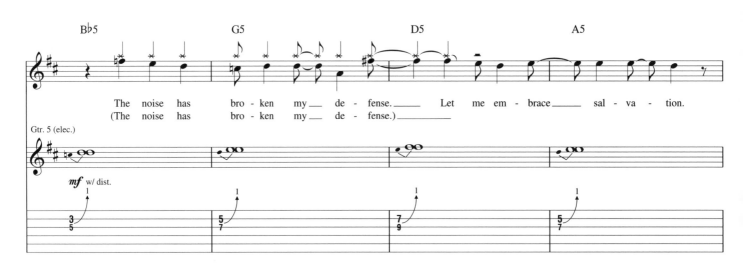

The noise has bro - ken my __ de - fense. _____ Let me em - brace _____ sal - va - tion.
(The noise has bro - ken my __ de - fense.) _____

Gtr. 5 (elec.)

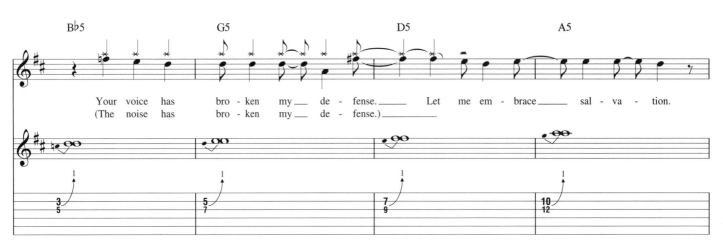

Your voice has bro - ken my __ de - fense. _____ Let me em - brace _____ sal - va - tion.
(The noise has bro - ken my __ de - fense.) _____

Let me em - brace, _____ let me _____ em - brace _____

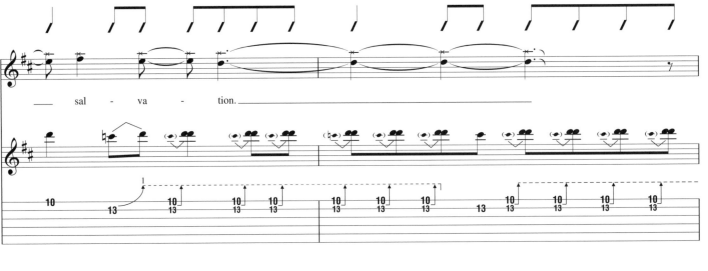

_____ sal - va - tion.

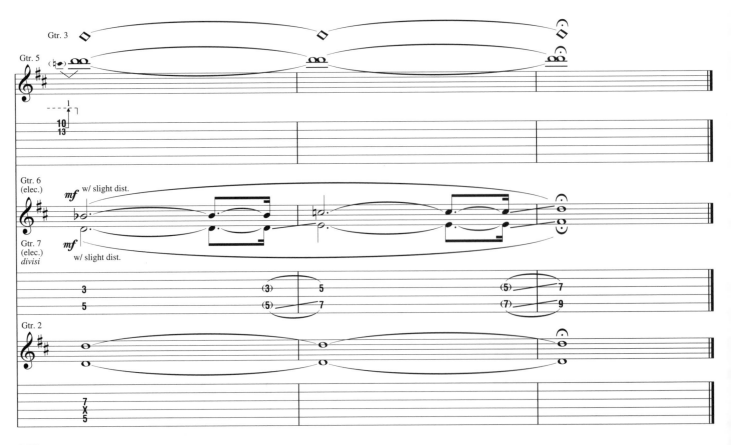

Getting Into You

Words and Music by Matt Thiessen

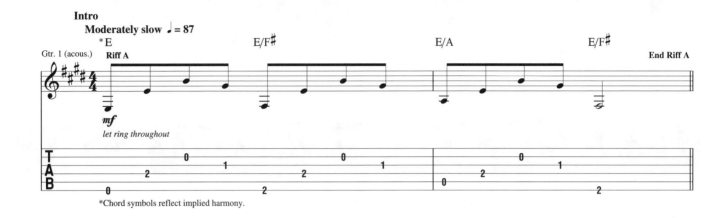

*Chord symbols reflect implied harmony.

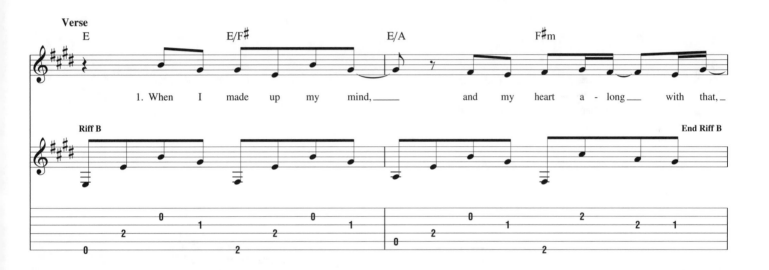

Verse

1. When I made up my mind,____ and my heart a - long____ with that,____

____ to live not for my - self,____ but yet for God,__ some - bod - y said,__

____ "Do you know what you are get - ting your - self in - to?"__

Gtr. 1: w/ Riff B (4 times)

E   E/F#   E/A   F#m

When I fi - n'ly i - roned out _____ all of my ___ pri - or - i - ties ___

E   E/F#   E/A   F#m

___ and asked God ___ to re - move the doubt ___ that makes me so un - sure of these ___

E   E/F#   E/A   F#m

___ things, I ask my - self, I ask ___ my - self, ___

E   E/F#   E/A   F#m

"Do you know what you are get - ting your - self in - to?" ___

Chorus

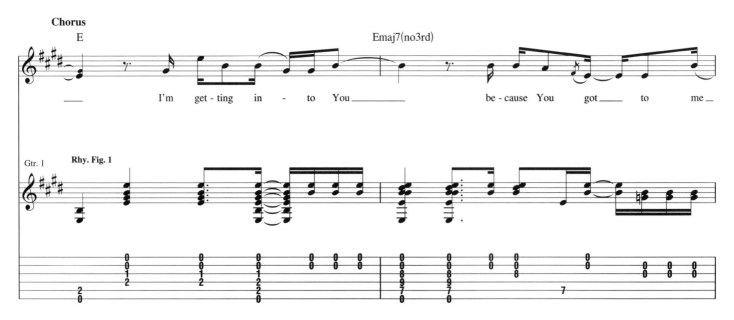

E   Emaj7(no3rd)

___ I'm get - ting in - to You _____ be - cause You got ___ to me ___

Gtr. 1   **Rhy. Fig. 1**

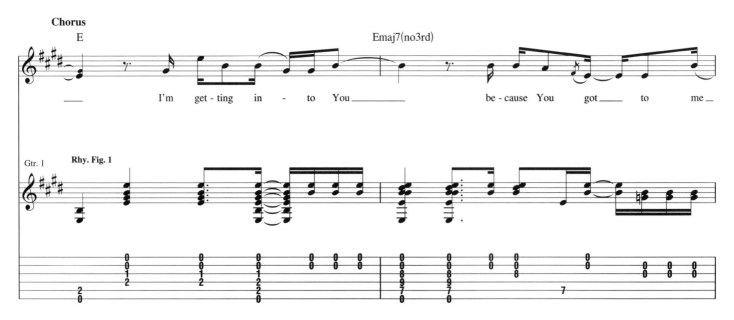

104

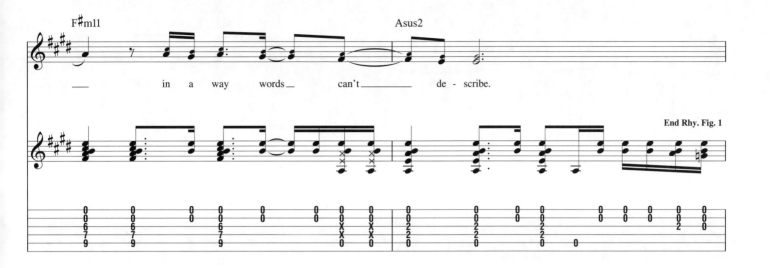

F#m11   Asus2

in a way words___ can't_____ de - scribe.

End Rhy. Fig. 1

Gtr. 1: w/ Rhy. Fig. 1

E   Emaj7(no3rd)

I'm get - ting in - to You_____ be - cause I've got___ to be.___

F#m11   Asus2

___ You're es - sen - tial to sur - vive. I'm gon - na love You with___ my_____

Interlude

Gtr. 1: w/ Riff B   Gtr. 1: w/ Riff A

E   E/F#   E/A   F#m   E   E/F#   E/A   E/F#

___ life._____

Verse

Gtr. 1: w/ Riff B (3 times)

E   E/F#   E/A   F#m

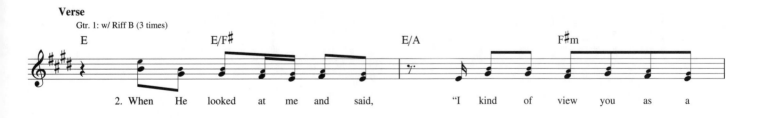

2. When He looked at me and said, "I kind of view you as a

E   E/F#   E/A   F#m

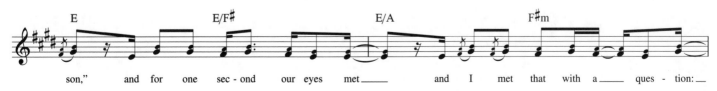

son," and for one sec - ond our eyes met_____ and I met that with a_____ ques - tion:___

"Do You know what You are get-ting your- self in-to?"

Chorus
Gtr. 1: w/ Rhy. Fig. 1 (1 3/4 times)

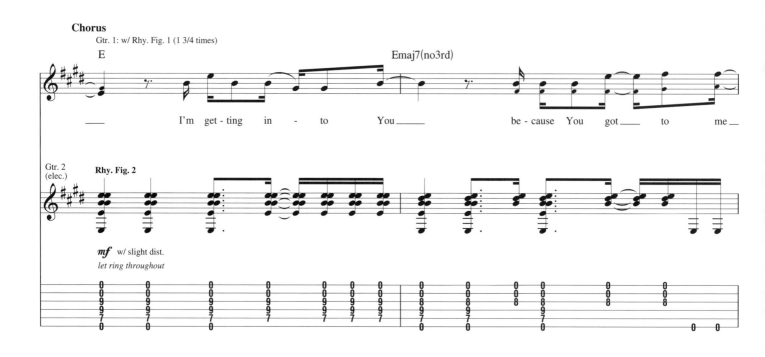

I'm get-ting in-to You____ be-cause You got____ to me____

Gtr. 2
(elec.) **Rhy. Fig. 2**

mf w/ slight dist.

let ring throughout

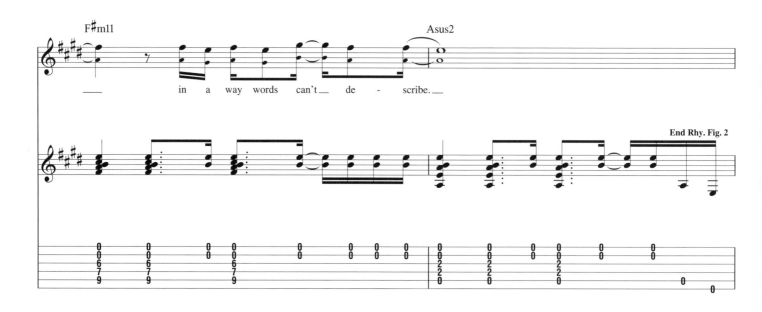

in a way words can't___ de- scribe.___

End Rhy. Fig. 2

Gtr. 2: w/ Rhy. Fig. 2 (1st 3 meas.)

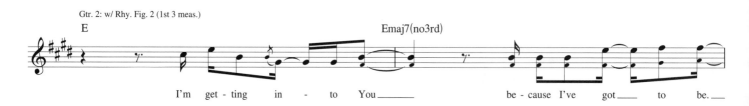

I'm get-ting in-to You____ be-cause I've got____ to be.

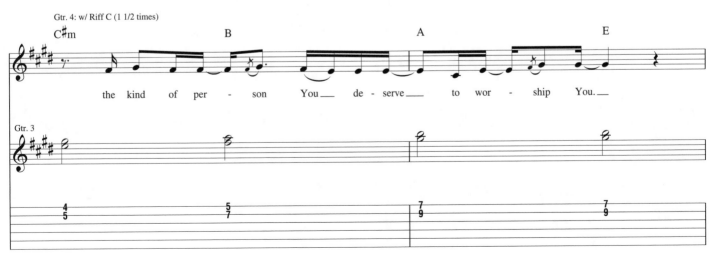

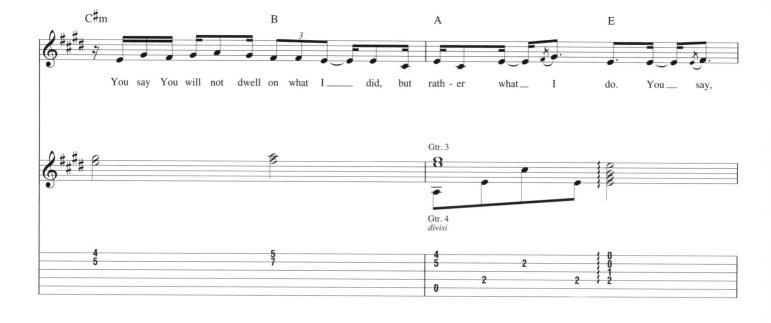

You say You will not dwell on what I ___ did, but rath-er what ___ I do. You ___ say,

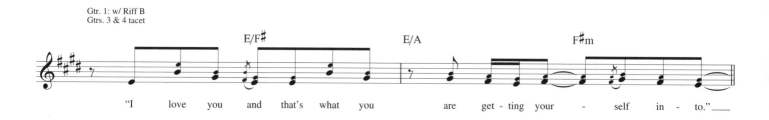

Gtr. 1: w/ Riff B
Gtrs. 3 & 4 tacet

"I love you and that's what you are get-ting your - self in - to." ___

Chorus

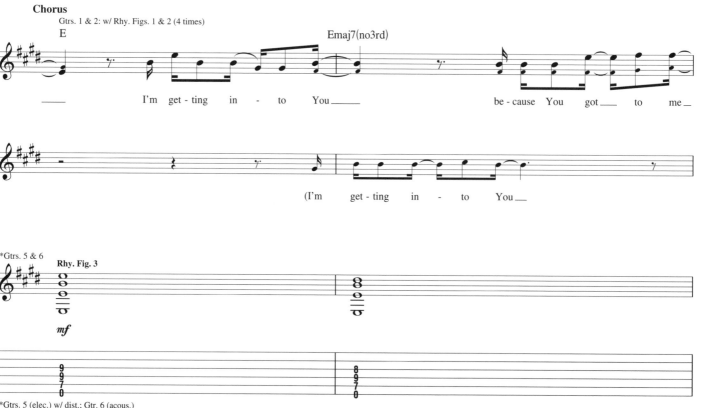

Gtrs. 1 & 2: w/ Rhy. Figs. 1 & 2 (4 times)

I'm get-ting in - to You ___ be-cause You got ___ to me ___

(I'm get-ting in - to You ___

*Gtrs. 5 & 6

Rhy. Fig. 3

Gtrs. 5 (elec.) w/ dist.; Gtr. 6 (acous.)

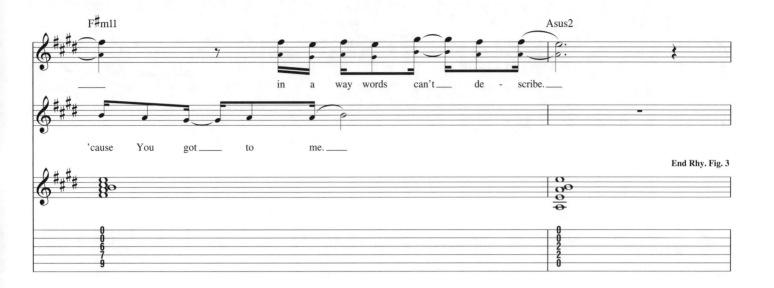

Gtr. 5: w/ Rhy. Fig. 3 (3 times)
Gtr. 6: w/ Rhy. Fig. 1 (3 times)

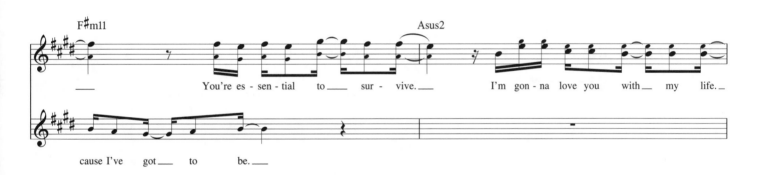

I'm get-ting in - to You____ be-cause I've got__ to be.__

get - ting in - to You,__ I'm get - ting in - to You__ be -

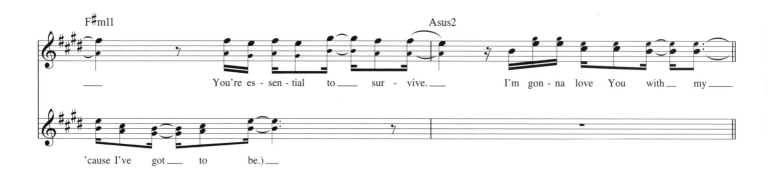

You're es - sen - tial to__ sur - vive.__ I'm gon - na love You with__ my__

'cause I've got__ to be.)__

Outro

Gtr. 1: w/ Riff B

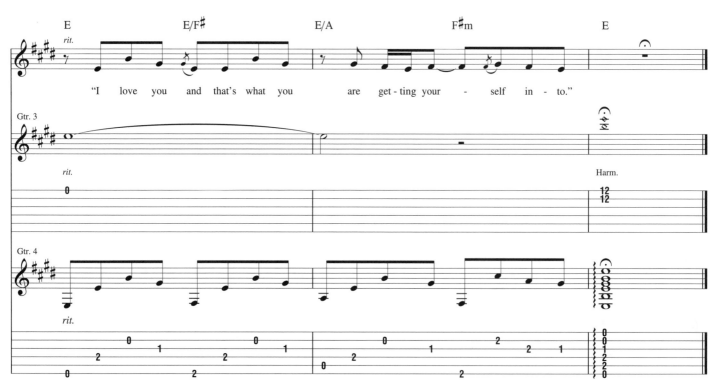

____ life.____ He said,

"I love you and that's what you are get - ting your - self in - to."

Gtr. 3

Gtr. 4

Harm.

110

Gibberish

Words and Music by Matt Thiessen

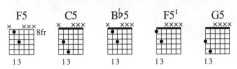

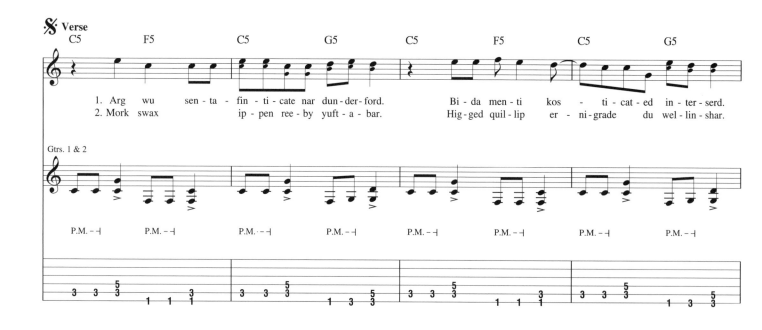

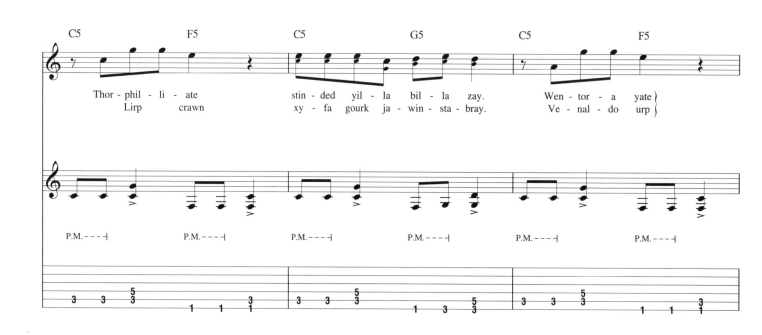

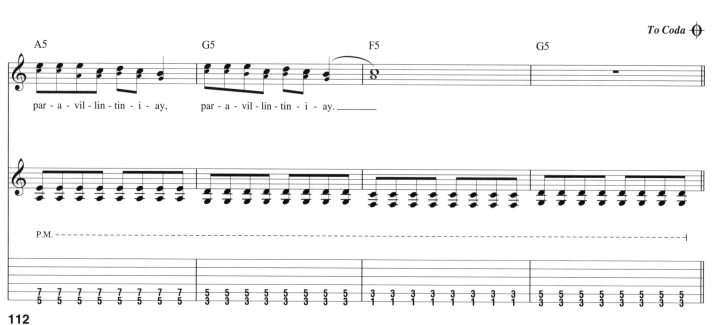

Pre-Chorus

Dor - ga or - pha dor - ga bil - la, dor - ga or - pha sti - fa - leare. Dor - ga or - pha dor - ga bil - la, ton - a - la - tion

(Gtr. 2, cont. in slashes)

Chorus

fo - na - mere. Stop talk - ing gib - ber - ish or just stop talk - ing.

Gtr. 1

Rhy. Fig. 1

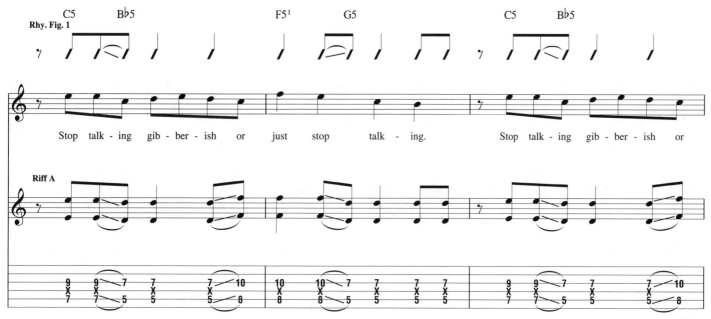

Stop talk - ing gib - ber - ish or just stop talk - ing. Stop talk - ing gib - ber - ish or

Riff A

just stop talk - ing.   Stop talk - ing gib - ber - ish or   just   stop   talk - ing

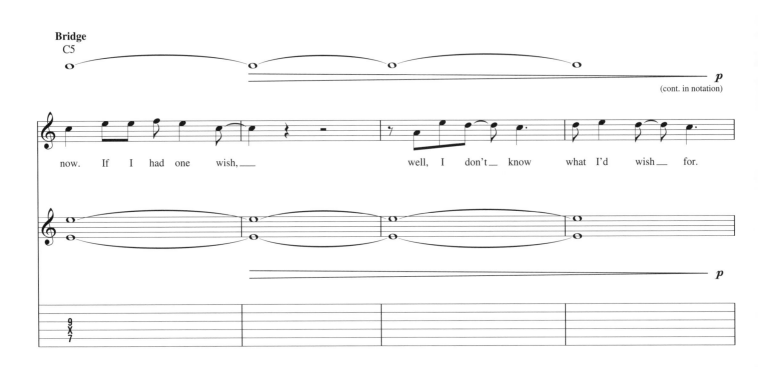

now. If I had one wish, ___   well, I don't ___ know   what I'd wish ___ for.

But if I had   a mil - lion zil - lion wish - es,   I'd use   one to let you

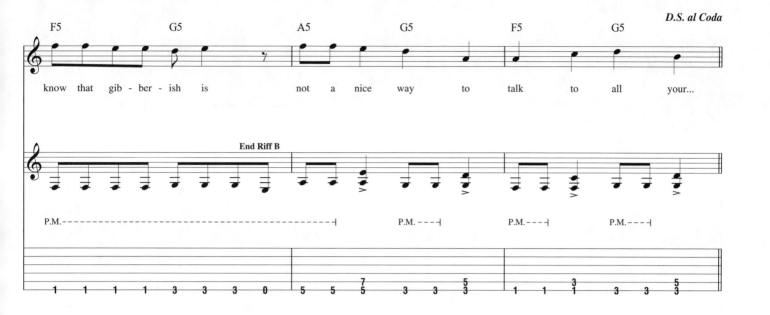

know that gib - ber - ish is   not a nice way   to talk   to all   your...

Coda

Chorus

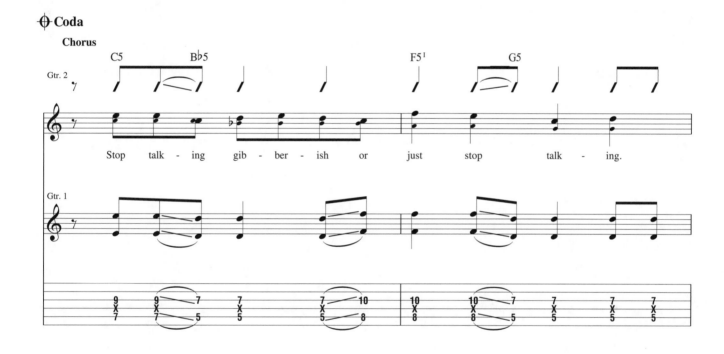

Stop talk - ing gib - ber - ish or just stop talk - ing.

Gtr. 1: w/ Riff A
Gtr. 2: w/ Rhy. Fig. 1

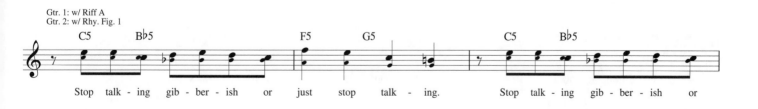

Stop talk - ing gib - ber - ish or just stop talk - ing.   Stop talk - ing gib - ber - ish or

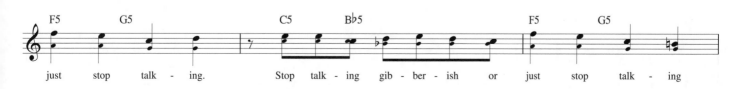

just stop talk - ing.   Stop talk - ing gib - ber - ish or just stop talk - ing

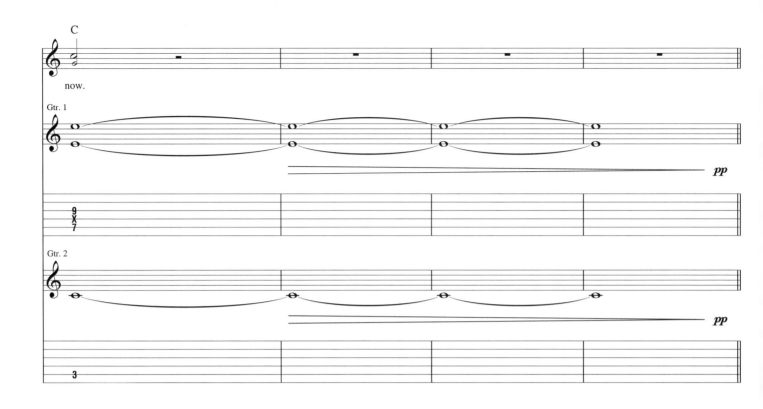

now.

Gtr. 1

Gtr. 2

pp

pp

Outro

Gtrs. 1 & 2 tacet

C5   F5   G5   C5   F5   G5

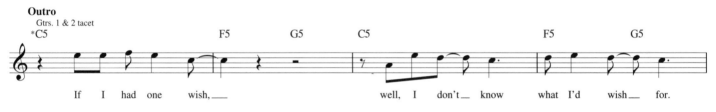

If   I   had   one   wish, ____   well,   I   don't __ know   what   I'd   wish __ for.

*Chord symbols implied by bass, next 4 meas.

Gtrs. 1 & 2: w/ Riff B

C5   F5   G5   C5   F5   G5

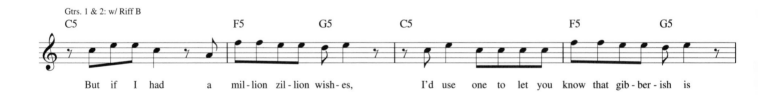

But if I had   a   mil-lion zil-lion wish-es,   I'd   use   one   to   let   you   know   that   gib-ber-ish   is

A5   G5   F5   G5   N.C.

not   a   nice   way   to   talk   to   all   your   friends.

Gtrs. 1 & 2

P.M. - - - - ┤   P.M. - - - - ┤   P.M. - - - - ┤   P.M. - - - - ┤

From End to End

Words and Music by Matt Thiessen

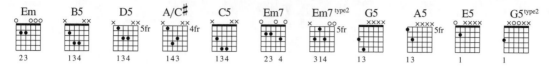

Intro
Moderately fast ♩ = 167

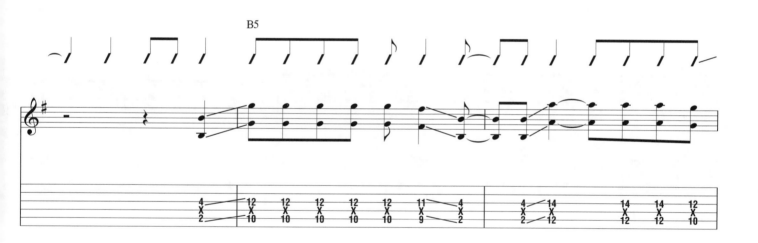

*Doubled throughout
**Chord symbols reflect overall harmony.
***Composite arrangement

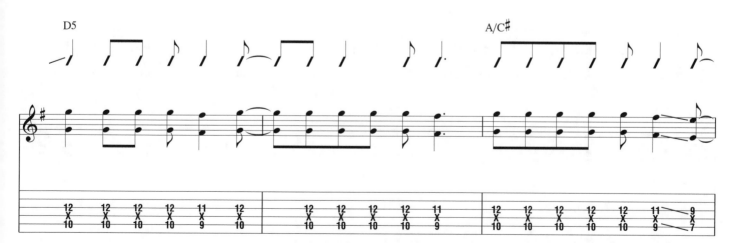

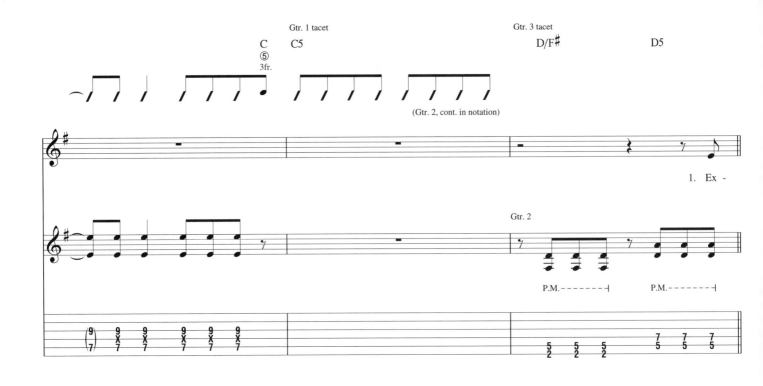

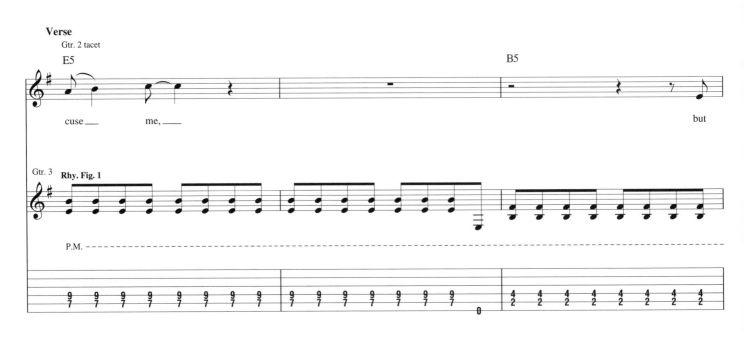

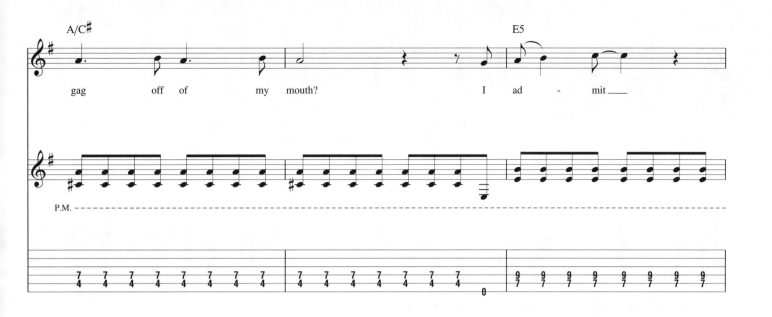

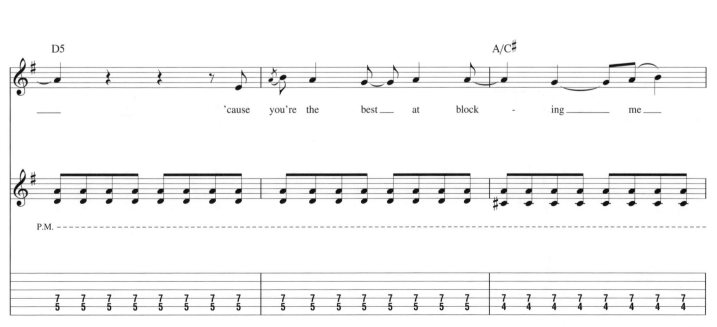

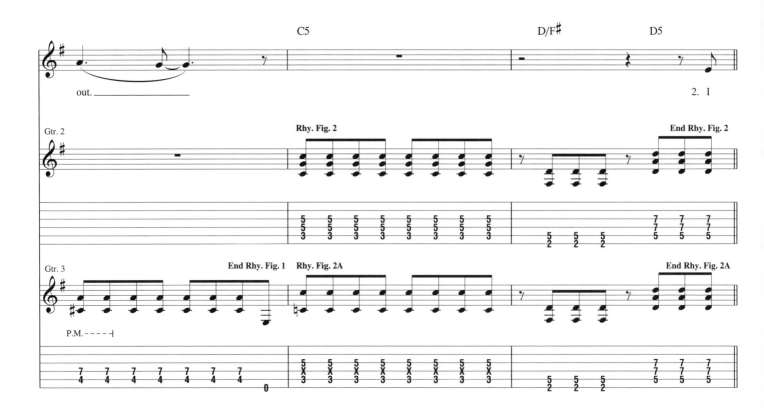

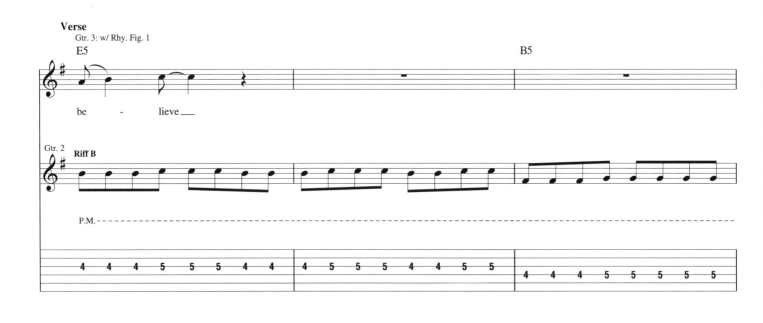

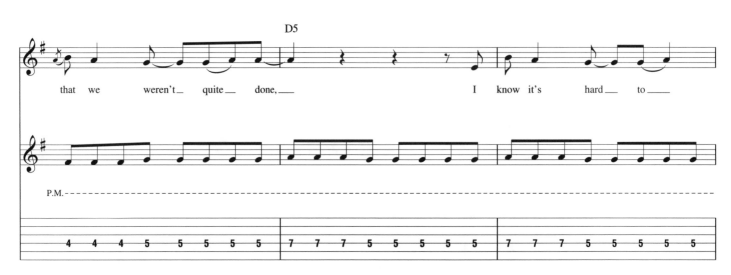

Pre-Chorus

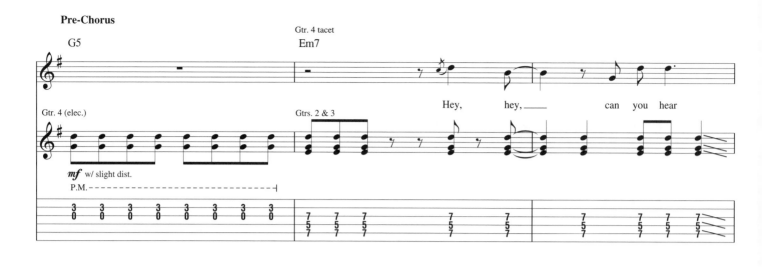

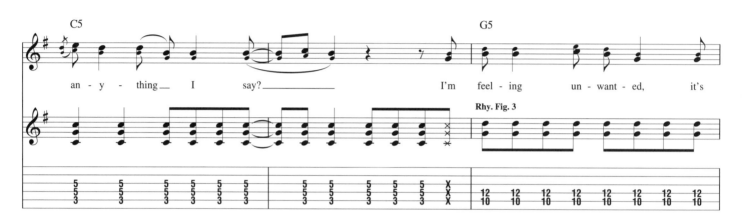

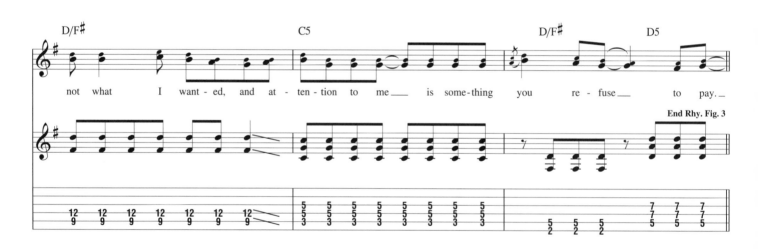

Chorus

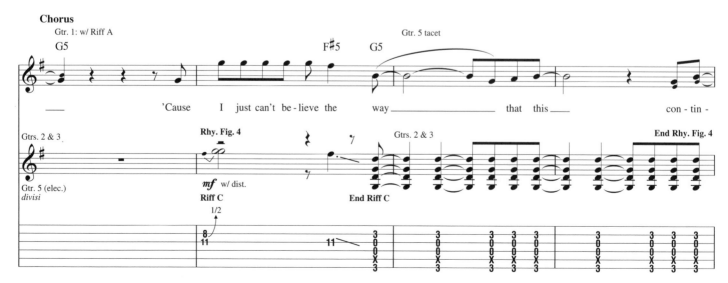

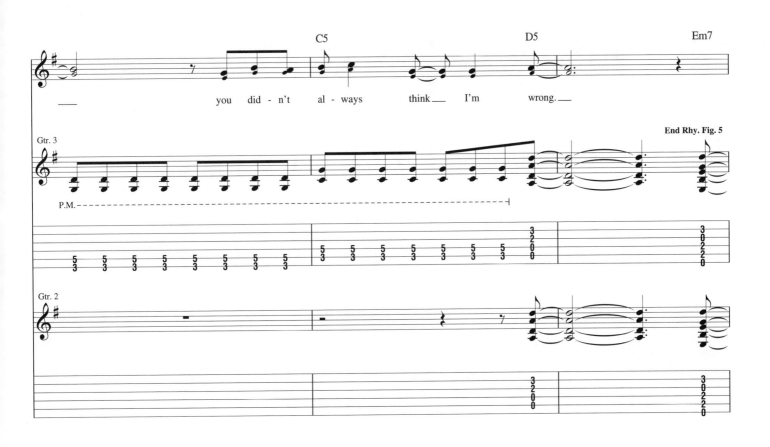

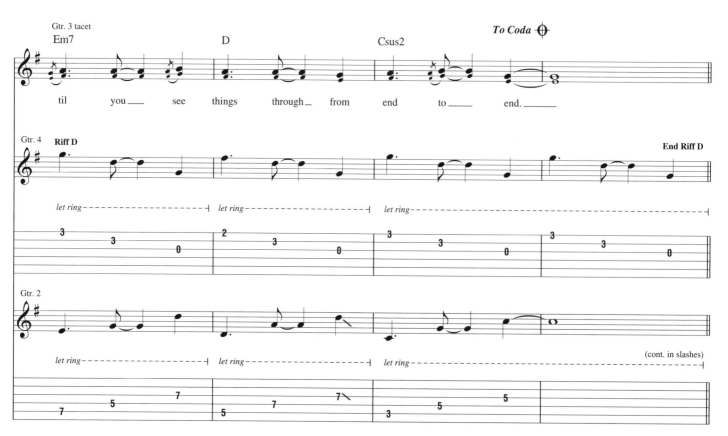

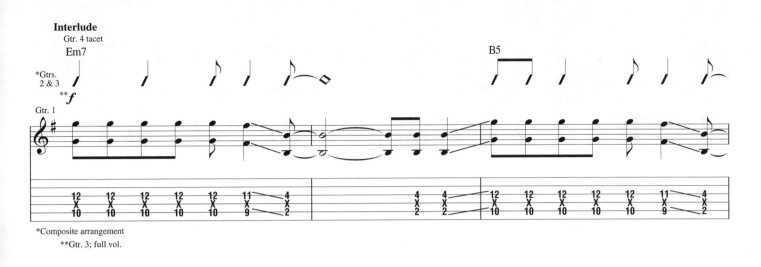

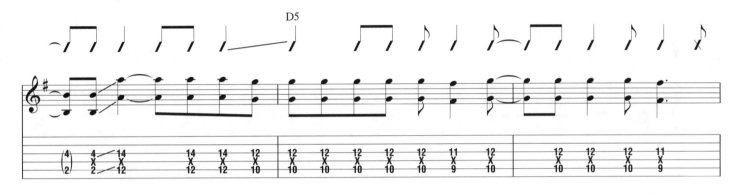

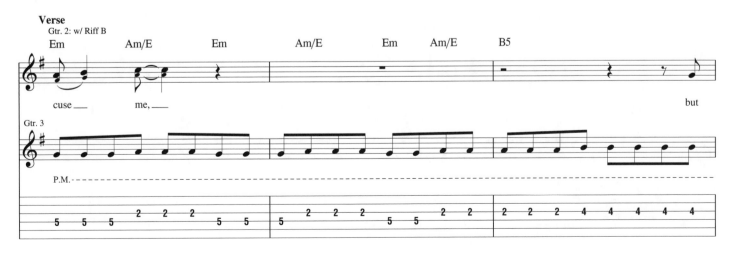

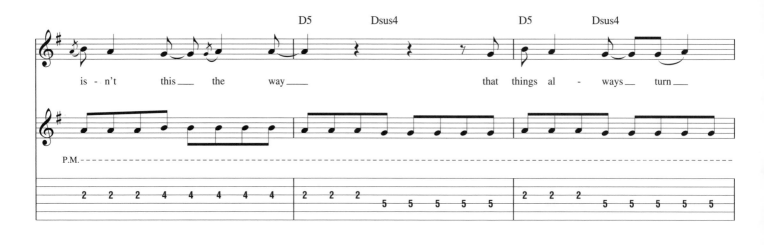

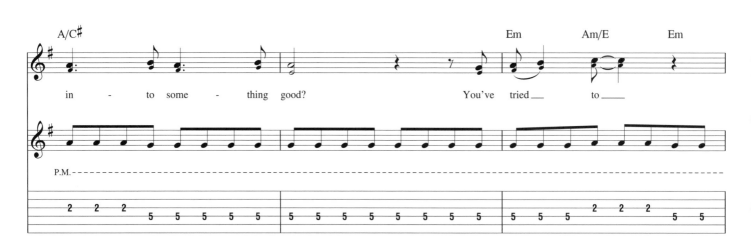

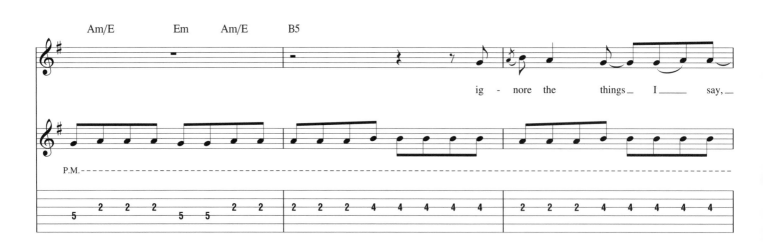

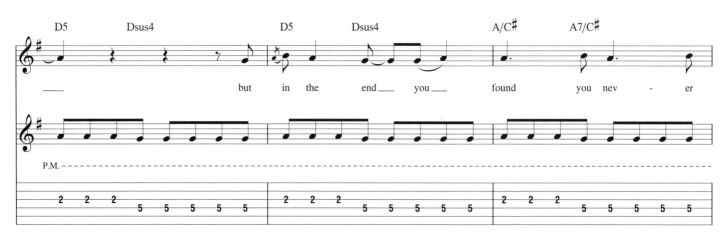

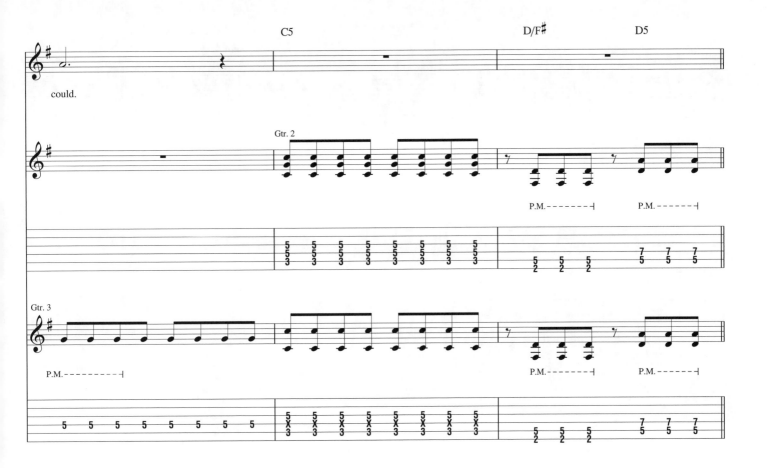

Pre-Chorus
Gtrs. 2 & 3 tacet

Hey, hey, ___ can you hear an-y-thing ___ I say? ___

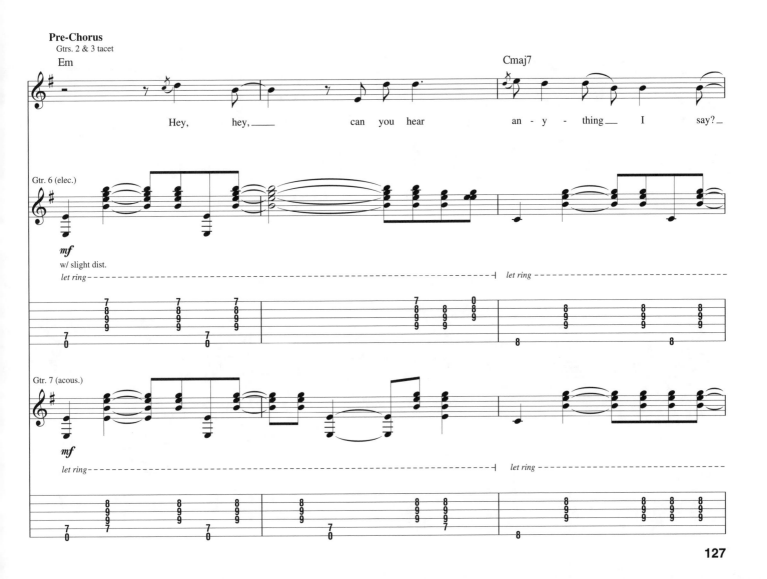

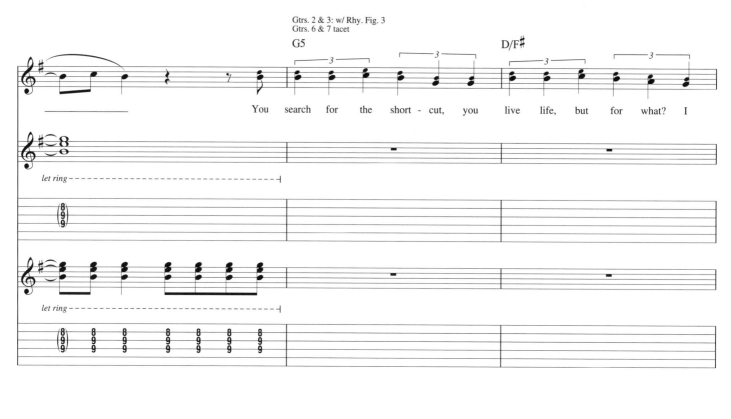

You search for the short - cut, you live life, but for what? I

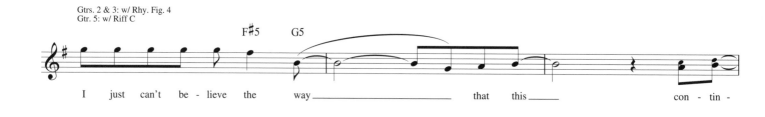

love you and hope you will find the truth___ some day.___ 'Cause

Chorus
Gtr. 1: w/ Riff A

Gtrs. 2 & 3: w/ Rhy. Fig. 4
Gtr. 5: w/ Riff C

I just can't be - lieve the way___ that this___ con - tin -

Gtr. 3: w/ Rhy. Fig. 5

- ues to___ go on.___ I say___ I wish___

D.S. al Coda

___ you did - n't al - ways think___ I'm wrong.

Gtr. 2

128

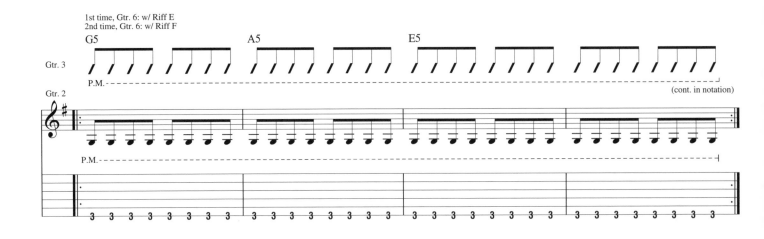

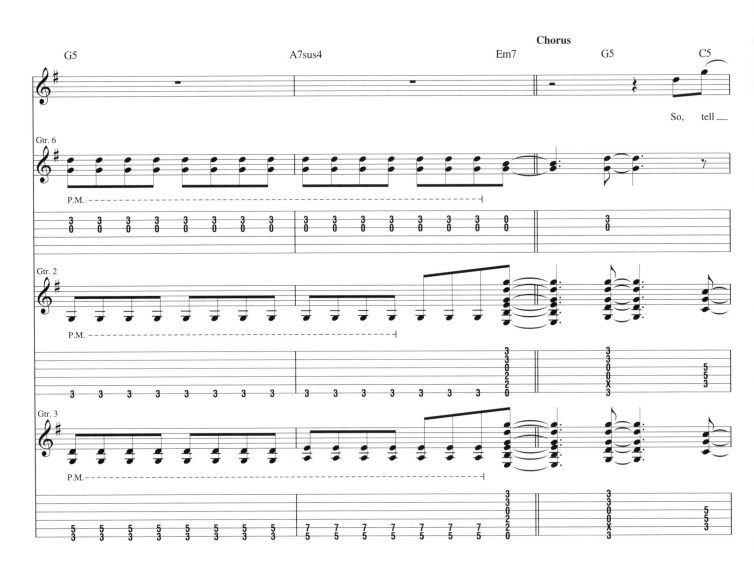

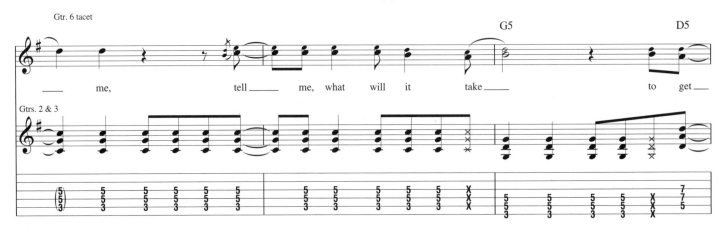

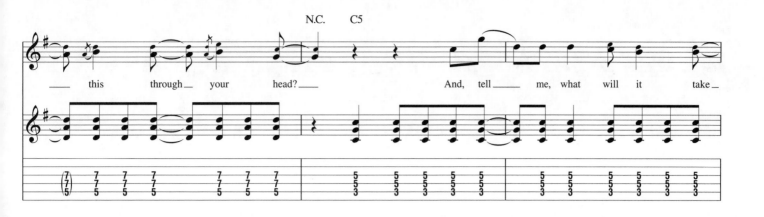

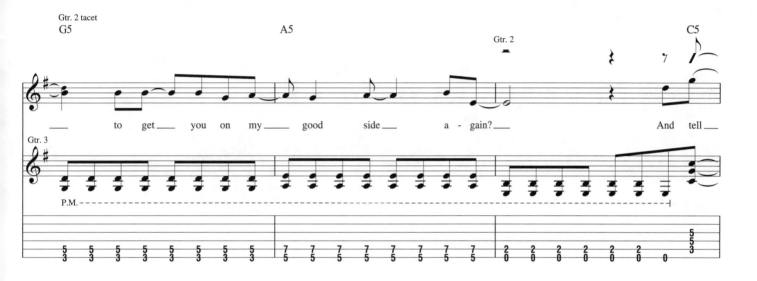

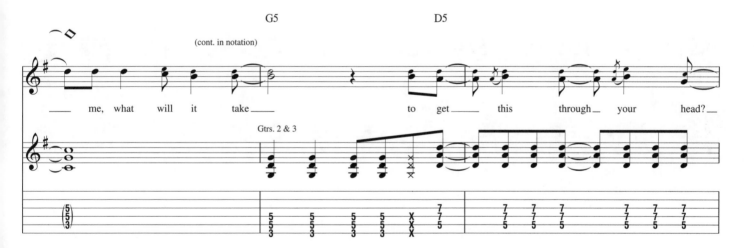

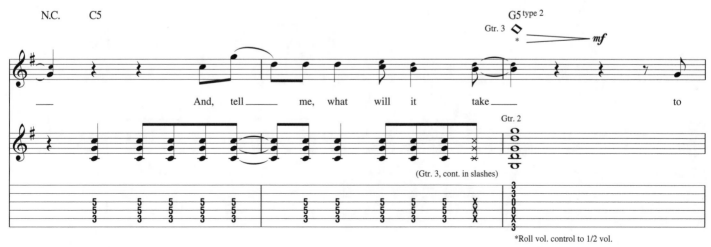

*Roll vol. control to 1/2 vol.

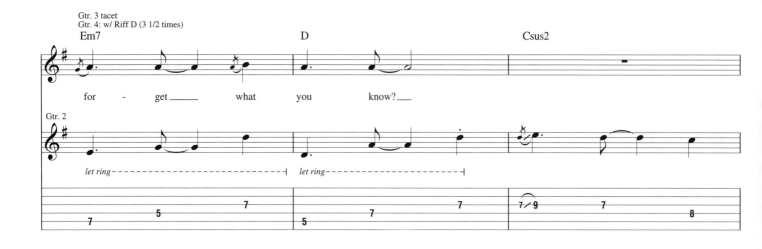

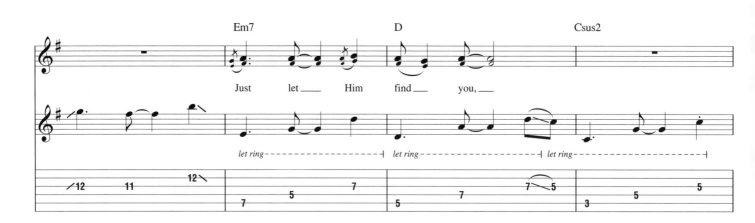

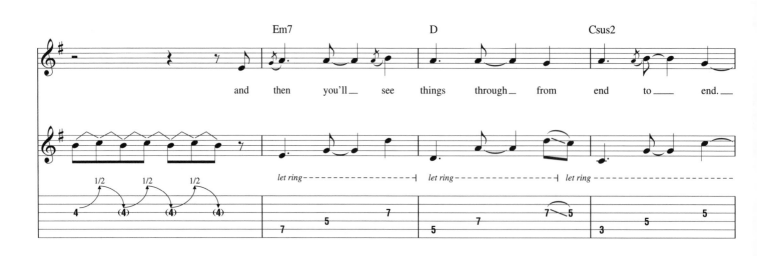

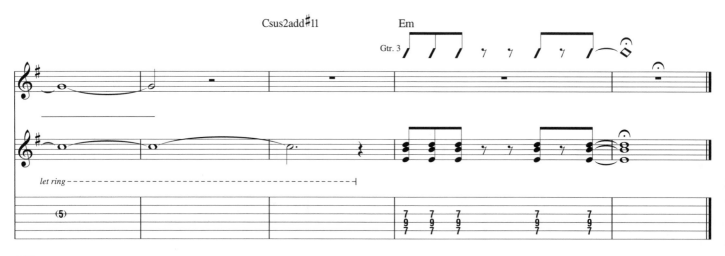

Jefferson Aero Plane

Words and Music by Matt Thiessen

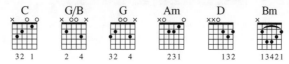

Gtrs. 1-3, 5 & 6 tuning:
(low to high) D-G-D-G-B-E

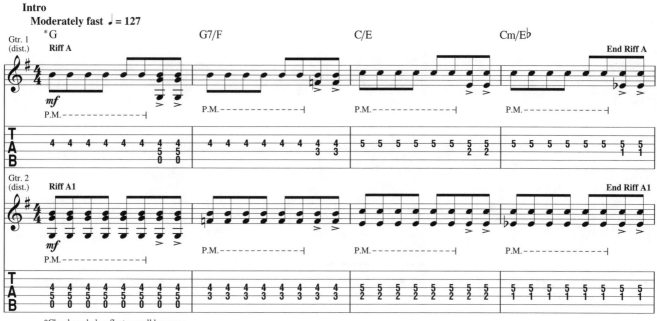

*Chord symbols reflect overall harmony.

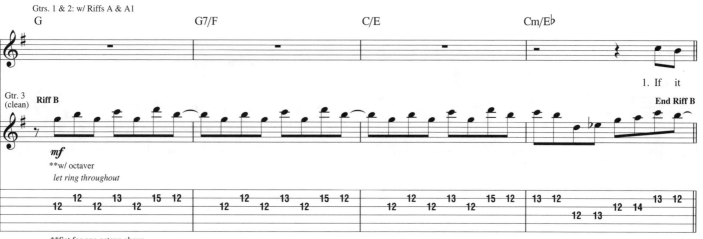

**Set for one octave above.

Gtr. 3 tacet

C/E   Cm/E♭

said noth - ing with flow - ers, though we al - ways talked for hours.___ And it seems___
save your plung - ing neck - line and kiss your face,___ you try to deck mine. If I be - have___

(12)

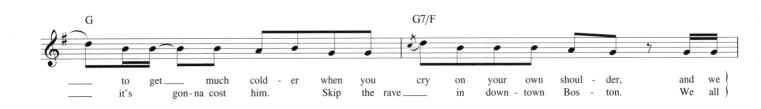

G   G7/F

___ to get___ much cold - er when you cry on your own shoul - der, and we
___ it's gon - na cost him. Skip the rave___ in down - town Bos - ton. We all

𝄋 𝄋 Chorus

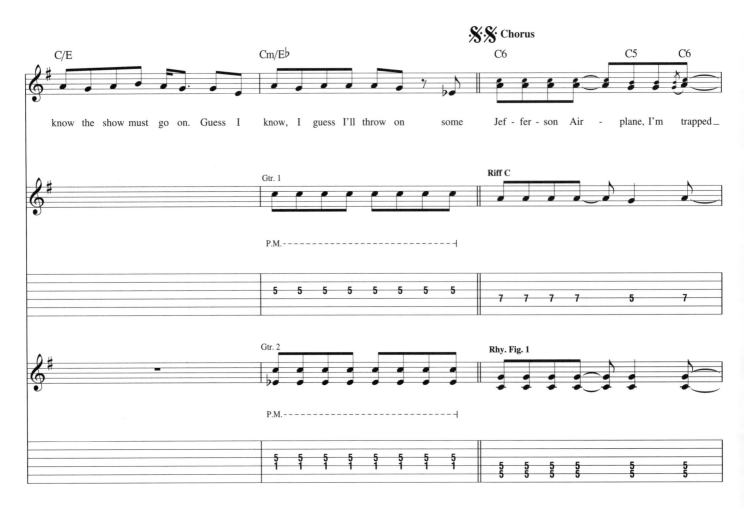

C/E   Cm/E♭   C6   C5   C6

know the show must go on. Guess I know, I guess I'll throw on some Jef - fer - son Air - plane, I'm trapped___

Gtr. 1   Riff C

P.M. -

Gtr. 2   Rhy. Fig. 1

P.M. -

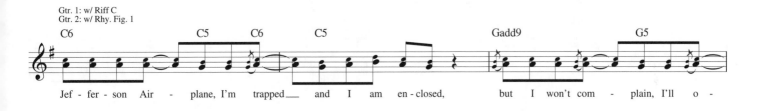

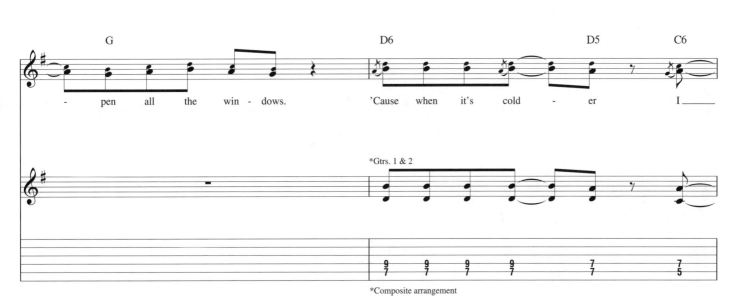

*Composite arrangement

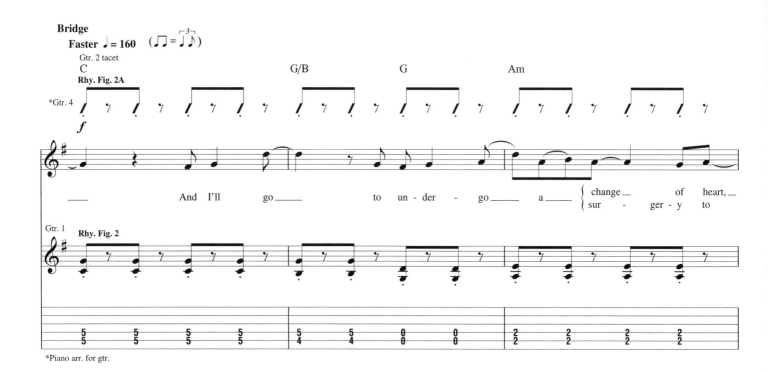

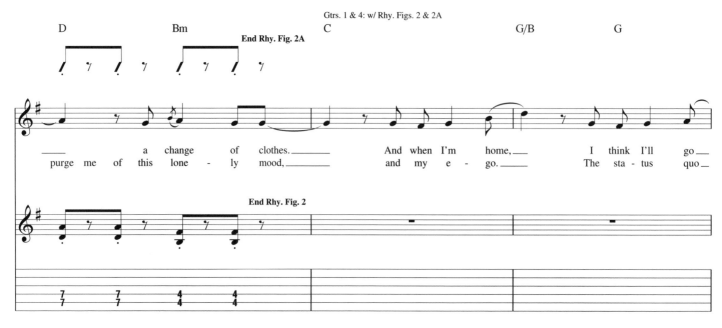

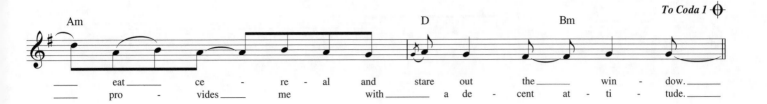

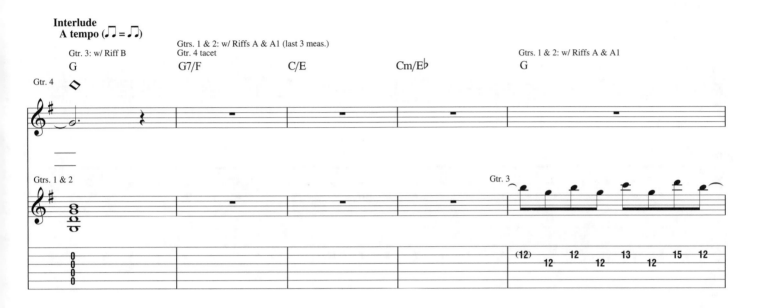

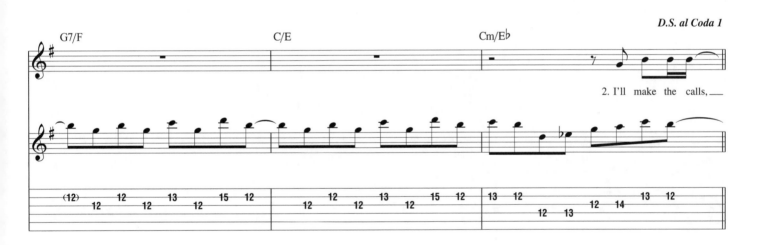

eat ce - re - al and stare out the win -

Bridge
A tempo (♫ = ♫)

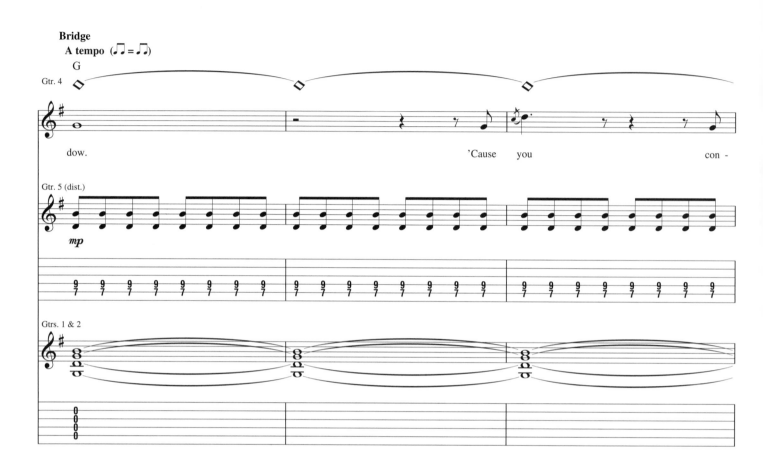

dow.   'Cause you   con -

fuse me more___ than an - y - one.   An ad - just - ment has___

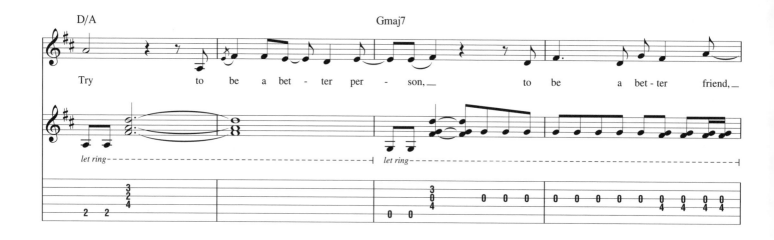

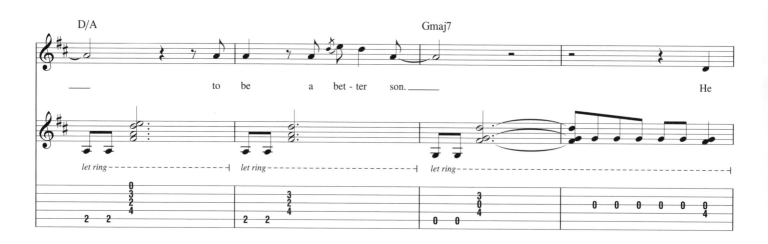

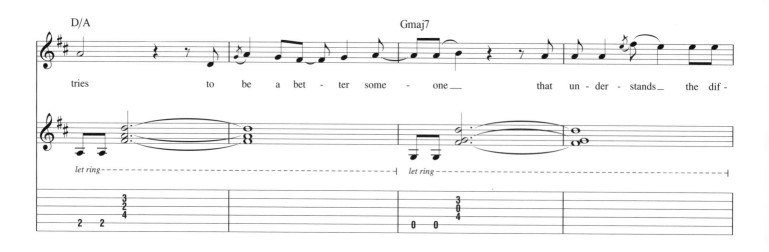

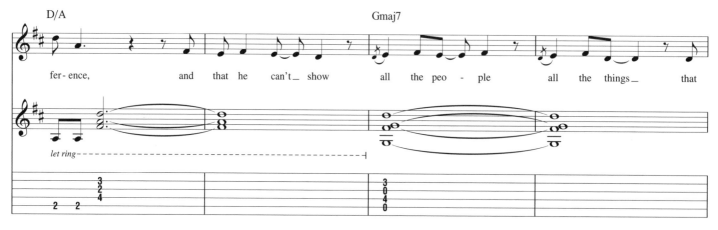

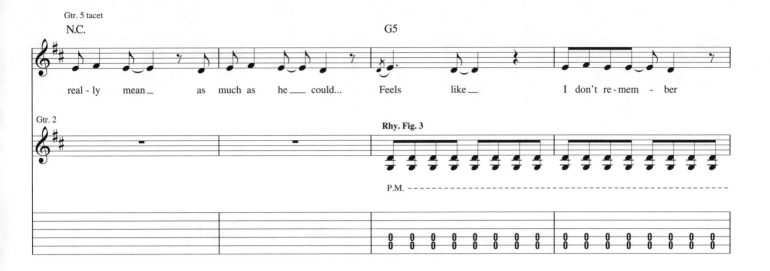

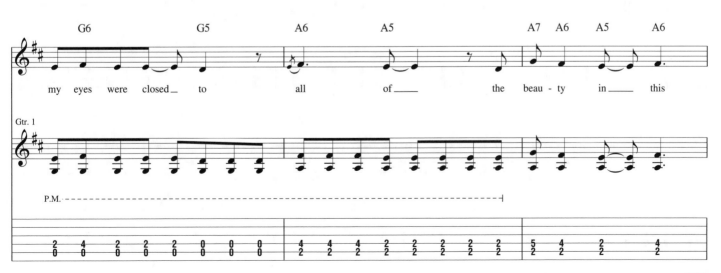

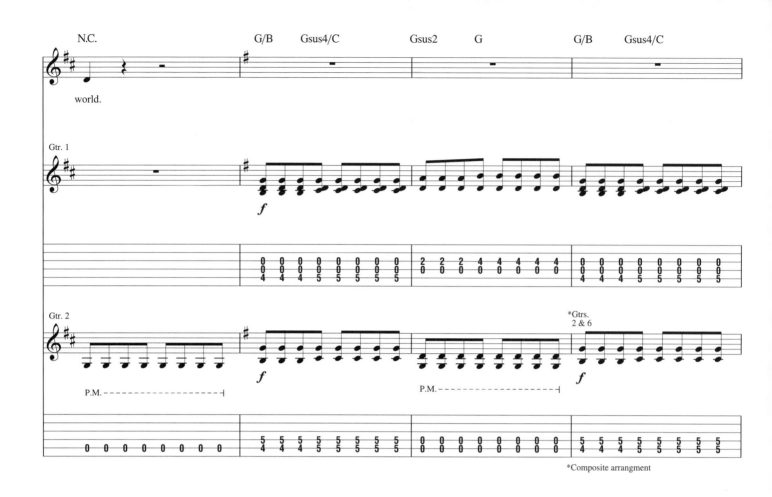

*Composite arrangment

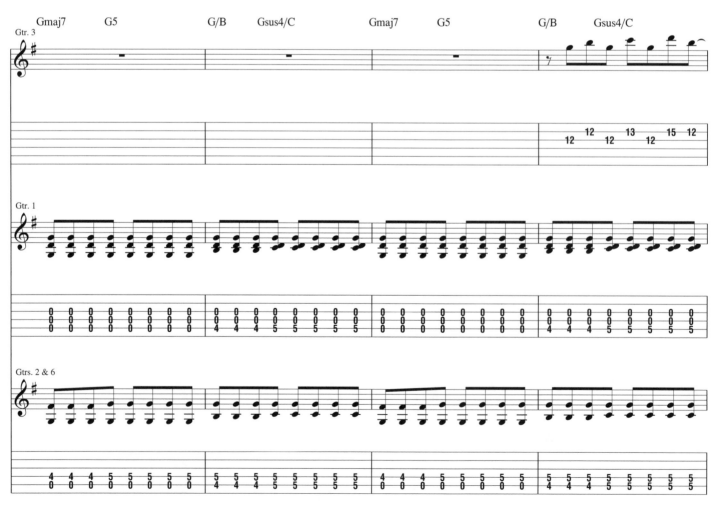

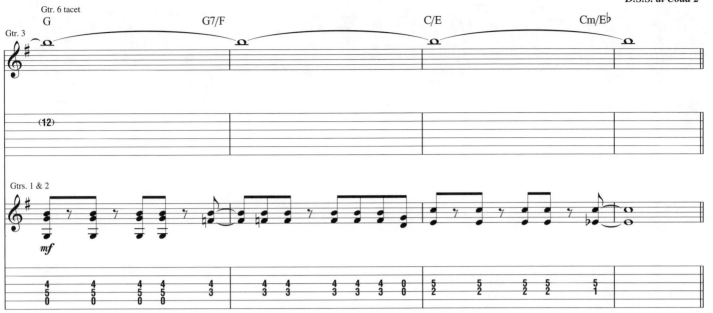

Coda 2

Bridge
Faster ♩ = 160

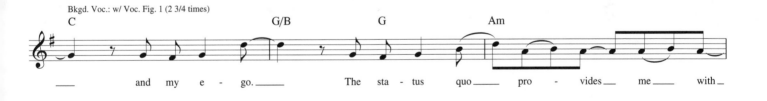

And I'll go ___ to un-der - go ___ a ___ sur - ger - y to purge me of this lone - ly mood ___

Voc. Fig. 1 — **End Voc. Fig. 1**

(Bop, bop, bop, bop, bop, bop, bop, bop, bop, bop, bop, bop, ah.) (Oo.) ___

Bkgd. Voc.: w/ Voc. Fig. 1 (2 3/4 times)

___ and my e - go. ___ The sta - tus quo ___ pro - vides ___ me ___ with ___

___ a de - cent at - ti - tude. ___ And I'll go ___ to un - der - go ___

___ a ___ change ___ of heart, ___ a change of clothes. ___ And I'll go, ___

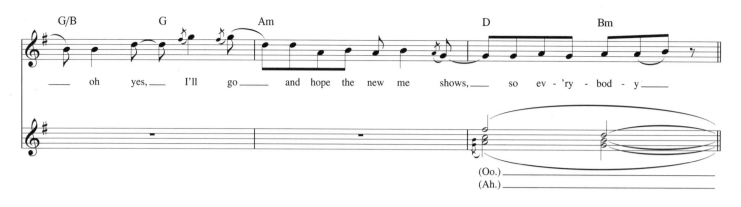

oh yes, ___ I'll go ___ and hope the new me shows, ___ so ev - 'ry - bod - y ___

(Oo.) ___
(Ah.) ___

Outro

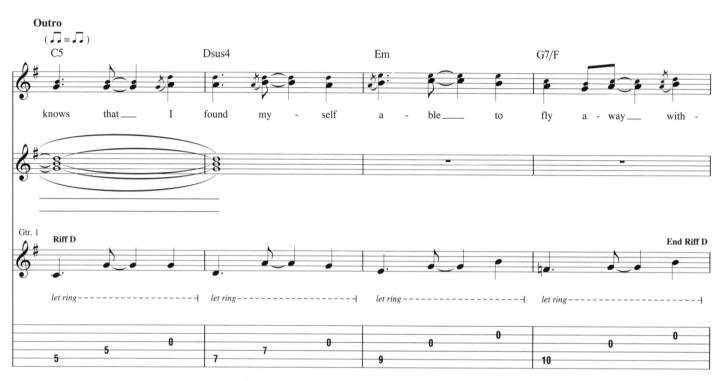

knows that ___ I found my - self a - ble ___ to fly a - way ___ with -

Gtr. 1 **Riff D**   **End Riff D**

let ring - - - - - - - - - - - ⌐   let ring - - - - - - - - - - - ⌐   let ring - - - - - - - - - - - ⌐   let ring - - - - - - - - - - - ⌐

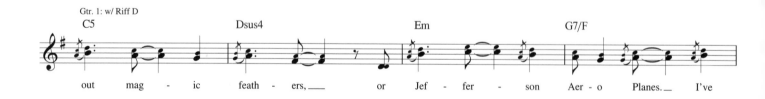

Gtr. 1: w/ Riff D

out mag - ic feath - ers, ___ or Jef - fer - son Aer - o Planes. ___ I've

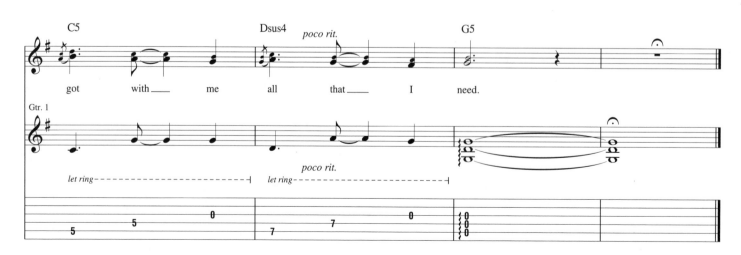

got with ___ me all that ___ I need.

Gtr. 1

let ring - - - - - - - - - - - ⌐   let ring - - - - - - - - - - - ⌐